MW00831072

BE YOUR OWN BANK

Be Your Own Bank

Hidden in Plain Sight

DYER BYTHEWOOD ROGERS

Be Your Own Bank Movement Publishing

Contents

Except the LORD build the house, they labour in vain that build it

Psalm 127:1
KJV

Acknowledgements

I'd like to thank God The Father, God The Son and God The Holy Spirit...for giving me the strength and vision to complete the process and stay the course.... All honor and Glory belongs to My Lord and Savior Jesus The Christ....

Gerald D Rogers
"The Visionary"

This book and the movement that it represents is a written representation of a life's work. As a tender 26 year old recent graduate who wrote a dissertation about Banks, it is so appropriate that I would end up here, with this mission, telling this story and impacting these lives with this information.

I would like to formally thank five women for motivating the acquisition of this knowledge, and igniting the passion for me wanting to communicate it to others. The first is my Mother. She raised me to read very early in my life, and set a standard of excellence that I was happy and proud to meet. Seeing her do it alone made me yearn to want to learn how to earn, and share it in turn.

The second, third and fourth young ladies are my beautiful, talented and intelligent daughters who are my ultimate "whys" for all that I do. The fifth young lady has become the behind the scenes coach of the coach, and provides a gentle, mentoring spirit that keeps me in check, and inspires me to want to be the best version of Dr. B that I can possibly be. She absolutely knows who she is.

Dr Craig Bythewood
"The Finance Doctor"

I'd like to thank God, my Lord and my Savior, for without him, nothing would be possible in my life. Thank you for this God breathed strategy, BYOB Cashout, that is changing lives around the world.

I dedicate this book to everyone that has been an influence in my life. There are a few that I must list specifically. My mother, Jacqueline Dyer "Jackie Faye", who kept me pressed for success. Terminally ill, raising three children, she helped me understand that success is yours and that my circumstances never dictated my reality. Only I determined what value my life would hold. After her transition into eternity, it's what I have held onto that has pushed me to never stop until I reach my goals. To my late grandparents, Willie and Lessie Curtis, Jr., who gave me a solid foundation. My late aunt Ora Hunt who taught me about entrepreneurship.

Special thanks to my children (TMD), Tiarra, Marquis, and Dasia, and granddaughter Tamera, I love you unconditionally. My sister Tanya Scott, "my favorite chick," my father Duane L Dyer, I thank God for you daily! Thanks to brothers Deandray Dyer and Terrance Scott.

Special acknowledgement to Sharon Tucker, "my second mommy," my aunt, Kim Curtis, "my sounding board," my aunt, Susan Leggett-Johnson, who at a young age showed me how to focus on the positive in life and always has proven herself to be someone in my corner. A special thanks to my aunts, Patricia West, Ora Stephens, and Millie Williams!

To C. Thomas Gambrell, I'd like to thank you for your leadership, coaching and your dedication to the BYOB Movement. #BYOBWORLDWIDE!! Gerald D. Rogers thanks for your mentorship, support and encouragement that has helped me stay focused. Dr Craig Bythewood, thanks for always keeping us grounded.

TO GOD BE THE GLORY FOR ALL HE HAS DONE AND CONTINUES TO DO!!

Tasha M Dyer
"TradeWhisperer"

Forward

When I was asked to share some introductory thoughts to this book I immediately said yes because I know the level of commitment the authors have to the betterment of the lives of others. In today's society's preoccupation with what I call "me-ism" it's a breath of fresh air to see people whose mission is to benefit others.

So when you read the words of this book please keep in mind that the only reason it exists is to make you and the life of your family better.

We are living in an extremely pivotal time in history. There is more worldwide societal instability than has been seen in over a century and yet there are other constants that continue to defy any and all circumstances that love be are the surface of media headlines. One of those constants is that even in these unsettling and uncertain times, some are continuing to financially prosper. While it may sound insensitive to say so, irrespective of that which grabs our collective attention, there are people whose financial security is *not* threatened even in the midst of the most troubling financial market circumstances. This is a fact. But there are reasons for this fact.

Some have inherited wealth and therefore live recession proof lives. But there is another more practical reason. There are people who have access to information that give them opportunities for financial success that others simply do not have. In the former you need family ties but in the latter you need an information pipeline. This pipeline is now available to you.

Traditionally employment and financial security was based upon the traditional path of getting a degree, then seeking employment in your field of expertise and learning through small businesses or large corporations. Most people found their careers as employees through small businesses. Small business creation is based on people willing to put their money at risk in the investment of an idea in the marketplace and if the idea is successful businesses are created and workers with the right education and skill sets are hired to fulfill the workforce based on supply and demand.

In decades past many people were able to work until retirement in one place of employment. But the market has drastically changed. Most people in today's economy no longer find the school to work paradigm one that guarantees success. And those who do find work are in many if not most instances not working in the fields for which they spent years in school. Not only that but now people may work five to ten different jobs in a lifetime. Sadly in many cases they are working two and three jobs at the same time to make ends meet. This creates an inordinate amount of stress that negatively impacts family life as well as ones personal health.

But there is an alternative and you have found it. In the pages of this book you will be introduced to information that can permanently change your life.

And it is this information that will allow you to excel irrespective of whether we are in a recession or a period of economic boom. Whether there is a bull or bear market.

This was not a misprint; this program will allow anyone to achieve financial growth irrespective of what the markets do! It is this information that most people have either not had access to or if they did, they lacked the access to capital to participate. That has changed!!

Tasha Monique Dyer, Gerald D Rogers and Dr Craig Bythewood have not only accessed this information but have now put it into a very readable, and practical presentation. Most importantly you don't have to be a millionaire to participate! Practically anyone can!

You will come to understand that financial success is available to all who are willing to understand the concepts and tools within these pages. But you will also be challenged. You will be challenged to examine yourself and ask yourself if you are ready to do something you thought only the rich could do. You will also be challenged to examine if you have self-sabotaging psychological behaviors and habits that perhaps have inhibited your success.

So the bottom line is this. If you are willing to commit to your own success and confront your own fears, there are untold financial possibilities ahead. Instead of having money in the bank, you will become your own bank.

Enjoy this journey with "Hidden in Plain Sight" as your guide.

John Allen Newman
Senior Pastor The Sanctuary at Mt. Calvary Church
Jacksonville Florida

Chapter 1

Mindset

Welcome to the Be Your Own Bank Movement: Information Hidden in Plain Sight! The Be Your Own Bank Movement is a philosophy that helps to transition the mindset and shift the financial paradigm helping to ensure you think like a bank, act like a bank, and become your own bank.

We are here because our parents were here and were exposed to the same information. You know the model: Go to school; get good grades; go to college, and get one of those good jobs. We have all done that, but we have to pose this question. Does that model create wealth?

None of us is different. We all started life with dreams, goals, and desires, and we have followed this path we were told was going to get us to a place called Success. We did it the way society told us to do it. That is why we can say that with confidence. We had the same parents and we all have heard the same information. Our parents did what they thought was right. As a result, we have gotten caught up in this cycle of life called the Rat Race. Now, we are so grateful that we are being exposed to different information.

Our new journey is to experience the shift that is going to happen in our lifetime! With this new information, we begin to operate with a new mindset: A transformation! Think back to when you were a child. You had a dream; you had a vision. You were told you could be and do whatever you wanted to in life. Then, as you grew, life happened, and dreams were put on hold. We learned that life required financial revenue and financial resources. I challenge you now to push pass that. Make the effort to push your mind in a way to not to stay stuck there! Your mindset has to transform!

As you begin this book, consider where you are. Ask yourself this question. Are you wealthy? Pause and really answer this question. Are you a billionaire? What does it really mean to you to be wealthy? Are you where you want to be Financially! You have to be definitive in what you desire.

Think about how being "wealthy" can change your life. Think about everything that you've ever desired, and all that you have ever wanted to accomplish in your life. Think about everything that a "wealthy" status could bring you. What would happen if you shifted your mindset just one degree?

For just one moment, shift your mindset to where you believe in yourself enough to believe that you are that wealthy person, that you are that "billionaire"! Imagine what that will do. See, that's the first step! You have to believe it first! Everything that forms everything, that becomes everything that is, it all begins with your mindset! So, your mindset is what you will become.

Whatever you believe that you are is what you will be. If you believe that you won't be, then you won't be. If you believe that you will, then you will. So, in this book, we are going to begin with your mindset. If you believe that you can, you will accomplish it. If you believe in your dreams, your goals, and your desires, that is what will be accomplished. So, as we begin, we have already established that you are a millionaire. You have declared and decreed that you are wealthy. With that declaration, it is important to understand the five mindset principles:

***

Mindset Principles

Why, Desire, Commitment, Being Coachable, and Belief. These mindset principles will remind you why you are here, why you purchased this book, and why you accepted the challenge to Be Your Own Bank!

The first principle is your compelling WHY. A why is your reason, your call, and your purpose. It must be compelling to you. We just talked about being definitive. We talked about making sure you understand what it is that you want. You have to get very specific with this thing! You have to know exactly what it is. You have to understand that your why has to make you cry. What can make you cry? What were you put on this earth to do?...to become? That is a compelling Why! You cannot be generic. It cannot be, "Oh, I just want financial freedom." Well, what is financial freedom? That is the same as saying, "I just want to be wealthy." Well, what is wealthy? Is it, "I just want to pay my bills at the end of the month," or is it generational wealth that you desire to create?

Why do you need to be specific? If you were having a conversation about a home purchase you were planning to make, you would state how many bedrooms and bathrooms you would need, what type of floors you would require, what floor plan you desired, whether you wanted a single-home or multi-unit home, etc. When buying a car you would have the same type of checklist. So when you discuss your finances and wealth you have to be just as definitive. Also, something has to drive you. Why are you doing this? Attach a purpose so meaningful that it brings tears to your eyes to your WHY and your desire for wealth. You're going to leave a legacy. The question is, what type of legacy are you going to leave?

The second mindset principle is your burning Desire. That is your internal fuel. It is inside of you. No one can put your flame out, but no one can give you this desire either. You must bring this desire to the table. Your burning desire is going to get you to overcome whatever obstacle confronts you. There is a quote that states, "You have to want success as bad as you want to breathe." Think about the power behind that statement. You need to breathe to live, but you do not have to concentrate to do it. You have become complacent, but that oxygen is a requirement for life. Now apply this to your financial life. Have you become complacent in your dreams and goals? Is your fuel still burning but dim? If someone were to take your breath away, you'd fight until your last breath to get it back. This is how you have to view success, your WHY and your DESIRE to obtain wealth....Be Your Own Bank!

Your third mindset principle is Commitment. Your commitment is your loyalty and your dedication that is non-negotiable. So often we are committed to our jobs, our religious organizations, our families, and so many other things, but you have to also commit to yourself. Think about the last time you traveled and were on an airplane. They so eloquently inform you that when the oxygen mask drops, you have to place the mask on your face first before you can attempt to help anyone else. That is because you need to help yourself to ensure you are in a position to help anyone else. How you do one thing is how you do everything, and you have to treat the rest of your life the same way. You have to commit to yourself first. We just talked about wanting success as bad as you want to breathe, wanting success, like you want that next breath. So, you have to want that commitment! You have to understand that if you are going to help someone, you have to first help yourself. Are you committed to you? Are you committed to becoming Your Own Bank?

The fourth mindset principle is Being Coachable. There is a yellow brick road to success. When you say you accept the challenge to be your own bank, are you ready to follow the steps and the process of the Be Your Own Bank Movement? You have already seen how the method that society has shown us does not achieve the necessary results for most. There are so many people reaching "retirement age" and still working. To reach the level to shift your financial paradigm, you have to take the necessary steps that are laid out for you. You might not understand it all initially, but, along the way, you will. You are here to become wealthy. Are you willing to take the information and the knowledge, and actively put it into action? Are you ready? Are you ready to say, "You know what? Today is my day. I'm going to read this book. I'm going to learn the market. I am going to learn how to be my own bank." It's not difficult; it's just different, and today is your day!

The fifth mindset principle is Belief. What do you believe to be true? Do you believe in yourself? Do you believe in the Be Your Own Bank Movement? Do you believe that you have what it takes? Do you believe in your WHY? Do you believe that you ARE a billionaire? ARE you wealthy?

These are the steps to get you there. This is your mindset. These are your mindset principles, and this is where it begins. Think it, believe it, speak it, become it! Have faith; say what you believe with no doubt, and it will happen. I am a MASTER TRADER, I AM THE SIGNAL, ALL MY TRADES END IN PROFIT! One million families will finally be educated and impacted through the Be Your Own Bank Movement!

Chapter 2

Subconscious Mindset & Your Quest

Our children will have a different mindset because we will have walked in a different paradigm. They are family members who will see someone that has developed a skill that is unlike what most our families have done before. We will feed off of that. There are families that will see what you are doing, ask what you're doing and become your business partners. There are individuals that are going to benefit because you thought enough of yourself to take control of your financial freedom.

This journey, The Be Your Own Bank Movement, and the opportunity that it presents to us is a chance to discuss each and every component of the economic empowerment pie that can help us to manage our business to a greater extent. When we combine the foreign exchange market with the cryptocurrency market, we're talking about 11.3 trillion dollars, but that still is only a slice of the pie. We are here to discuss that and also to make sure that we are comfortable with every single slice of the economic pie: personal finance, economic empowerment, being your own bank, understanding and managing how this market works, and understanding and managing all of the tools we can use.

I teach a class called NLP, neuro-linguistic programming. *Neural* obviously is a Latin term, which represents the brain-neurons, neurologists, neurological, anything involving the brain. For instance, a neurosurgeon is someone who operates on the brain. *Linguistic* means language. A linguist is someone who studies language, like so neurolinguistic, (define this term here). Finally, the word *programming* simply means putting together a process. So, the bottom line is that neuro-linguistic programming is a method for learning to tap into one's own subconscious mind in order to operate at a higher efficiency. But neuro-linguistic programming can also be used to tap into other people's subconscious as well, connecting with them in a way which allows you to influence or motivate them or get them to see things differently, without all of that conscious stuff such as resistance, opinions, and beliefs getting in the way.

Consider this: When we are in a situation where we have an opportunity to go to the next level of something, oftentimes, things come up that stand in our way, things that we do not realize are there. If we think back, say maybe the last ten times you tried to accomplish something that you may have had an issue with, you will find that there is a pattern. There is a pattern of subconscious self-sabotage. This means this issue rests far below your ability to think. There-fore, you do not even realize that you are not aware. So, while we are spending our energy learning this skill, make sure that we are learning the BYOB Cashout Strategy. Make sure that we are doing everything in our power to study and learn this skill to the best of our ability.

It is natural and it is normal for some things to come up that we may not be aware of, for some things that come up are resistance. So, what I would like for you to do is this: Think about the fact that if you are experiencing some re-sistance, if you're experiencing some scenarios that keep re-peating and that keep you from getting to the next level in terms of your trading and learning this skill, then rec-ognize that this is par for the course. In fact, we can even explain this by using a market term, one we often come in contact with in the foreign exchange markets. Think about how many times we talk about the overall trend of the mar-ket changing directions. Think about how many times we think about a buy pattern changing into a sell. Think about how many times we talk about a sell pattern changing into a buy.

Now, what makes this happen is simply a collection of buyers and sellers tugging against each other, which then creates a new pattern. However, one of the things you have to recognize when we talk about resistance in foreign ex-change, is that it is simply a market getting to a certain point and then falling back, and it keeps falling back and keeps falling back until, eventually, it will bust through the plateau and then shift. Almost every rule that we look at in the be-your-own-bank cash out, as we navigate in the foreign exchange, revolves around being able to notice and identify a shift in direction. Understand, however, that in markets terms there is always a resistance first, and then a market move. Know that in your emotional life, in your spiritual life, the same exact thing happens on your way to your breakthrough, on your way to your incline, on your way to your ascension! There is always going to be some resistance, so, rather than having an issue with it, rather than having a problem with it, rather than criticizing yourself because of it, understand that that's just the way it happens and that it happens like that on purpose. Understand that sometimes the bigger the resistance, the bigger the opportunity for you to grow! Know this: If you are doing something new and it is easy, if there is no resistance, you are probably not going to get a lot out of it. Because it is the resistance that provides the signal that this is something that can be big for you. If you are driving around in your car and you see that Check-engine light, you are not going to just cover it up and keep driving. Instead, you are going to recognize the signal and realize that there is something that needs to be addressed. Look at your resistance points the exact same way because the resistance is the Check-engine indicator. The resistance is the signal that you are about to do something big, and the bigger the resistance, the bigger the paradigm shift, and the larger it can be in your benefit.

When I started learning to drive a manual transmission car, I had to recognize that there was a skill set that I was developing, just like the skill set we are developing now. In order for me to put the car into first gear on a hill, I had to be very careful with my foot placement, and I had to really take my time for it to work. I had to recognize that every time I put it in first gear on a hill, I would rock back. I would have to rock back in order to go forward. This is very rele-

vant to where we are right now. In the beginning I thought
the rock back was an issue and because it was rocking back,
I thought I was doing something wrong, so I would hit the
gas and the car would stutter. It wasn't until I accepted the
rock back and recognized that I had to rock back in order to
get it into first gear BECAUSE I was on a hill. I needed the
rock back to get the momentum to be able to put it in first
gear. Something else that I noticed was that the steeper the
hill, the bigger the incline, the bigger the rock back. The
bigger the incline, the bigger the rock back, the bigger the
opportunity for me to grow and to reach another paradigm.
So I said all that to say this: Resistance is a signal in the
market to tell you that something is about to change direction. The same thing happens to you when you experience
a "rock back." That resistance, the pattern that you keep
experiencing, that is your signal. That is your indicator that
you are about to blow up.

So, whatever rock back you are experiencing with this
skill, whatever rock back you are experiencing in your life,
whatever rock back you are experiencing in an interaction
with somebody, know that nobody has the ability to climb
into your head and push your buttons. You are allowing
your buttons to be pushed. If we shift our perspective and
instead of looking at it as what they are doing, looking
at them as being a problem, looking at it as being an issue,
looking at this as a rock back, just understand that this is
the necessary step for us to get to where we need to go.
Some of you really may be doing a really good job in 20 areas of your life, but that 21st area is your ability to be able
to handle the rock back and your life projection.

Our ability to trade is going to be intensified by the
mood we are in, our emotions. We want to be able to exude

a peaceful emotion so that we can trade calmly and smoothly. If we are in a position where we are upset with someone else, our outlook will be swayed by this; that affects our ability to trade. This affects our ability to be able to recognize the power of the rock back. You must shift your emotions to learn to love from the inside and own your reactions. The two most dangerous phrases in your quest to be spiritual are "but she" and "but he". It is so easy to place your focus on what someone else is doing or saying. When you do so, you are using that as an excuse to look at what somebody else is doing instead of owning your reaction. We have zero control over what other people do and say, but we have a hundred percent control on how we respond. This is a slightly non-financial issue I'm talking about right now, but it has a lot of application to our finances because finances are very emotional. If you are feeling off balance and you are not feeling centralized, it affects your ability to be able to make good financial decisions.

There is value in your understanding that the way in which you manage those rock backs around you from a relationship perspective is to recognize that there is only one thing to look at, and that is YOUR reaction, how YOU responded. There is an example that reinforces this that I talk about a lot. I call it the ping- pong-ball analogy. I want you to think about this somewhat as an individual; whether it is you or the other person doesn't matter because then that is to say someone has a message. Did they want to send to you? Let's just make it be the other person so we can look at us. If somebody wants to send a message to you, suppose they take that message and they write it on a ping pong ball. Now what is supposed to happen is that person throws you the ping pong ball. Then you catch the ping pong ball, look at it to read the message, and subsequently receive the message. Maybe that message can make you better. Maybe that message can give you a growth opportunity. Maybe that message is something that has been said to you for years and you have not taken action. Maybe that message can make you a better person, a better parent, a better spouse, a better human. All you have to do is catch the ping pong ball and read the message. But what we do when we see that ping pong ball approaching us is totally different. What we do is pick up our defensive paddle and hit that ball right back. If you immediately hit the ball back, that means you never had the opportunity to view the message.

If you think about it, many people are doing this, and when there is an argument, nobody is receiving the message from the other person. All we are doing is hitting it back with our defensive paddle. This is not in any way telling you about who is right or wrong. That is irrelevant. What I am talking about is the fact that we keep hitting this message back to the other person. Both sides are hitting the message back and nobody is taking the time listening to the other. When someone is speaking, instead of receiving what they are saying, we are thinking about what we are going to say next. So, the spouse, the banker, the business partner, the person at your job, the child, they have something to say, but you are not listening to them, because you are too busy figuring out what you are going to say. I am challenging you, in your own your response, to take responsibility for how you feel about what they are saying. Put the paddle down. Catch the ball. Look at the message. This message is not for others, it is for you. This message is for you because you do not have a way to make somebody else read the message.

That is not your goal. Your goal is to do it because you are the only person that can receive this analysis. Somebody else is not going to be able to receive it. You have to receive it. So, if the message is coming to you and you catch it, you stopped the pattern, and you received the message without defensively sending it back.

If you do this a few times with someone who is non-responsive, eventually they will start to realize, wait a minute, there is a new pattern here. Even though they do not immediately give a response, they actually listened and by listening, you know that the pattern stopped. It only takes one person to receive the ball. If you start being the person that receives the ping-pong ball, instead of hitting it back, eventually it is going to make that person relax and be able to communicate. There is a loved one right now that you are having arguments with just like this, and you are so focused on what they are saying, on what they are doing, or what they are not saying or doing, instead of focusing on your reaction. So all you have to do is to be that person to receive that ping pong ball and say, you know what , let me look at my reaction.

We have covered several topics that are very important to what we are doing right now. We have talked about the fact that the rock backs— the resistance, the things that are going on in your life, that are coming up right now—are normal. Not only are they normal, but they are the signals that let you know you are moving in the right direction. In fact, the bigger the rock back, the bigger the resistance, the larger the paradigm shift is going to be when you get to the other side of it. We need to have this balance in order to be in a position to maximize our economic empowerment, and especially to be able to trade effectively. So one of the ways we get there is, instead of pointing at what other people are doing and saying, we focus only on our reaction.

Another thing that is important to understand as you transition into this understanding, is to understand that who a person is more important than what they say or do. So think about how many people you could benefit from, if you put who they are above what they say or do. Spouse, parent, police officer, teacher, supervisor—who that person is, is more important than what they say or do. So, by understanding the fact that we are only responsible for our reaction and by focusing on how we respond, we automatically bring peace and balance into our lives and put ourselves in a better position to do what? To learn this skill, to understand the power of the rock back to recognize the resistance is a signal for us to do better, to be our own bank and to continue to grow and prosper in every way.

Chapter 3

Stages of Learning & the BYOB Movement

Why are we so excited about the individuals represented in the Be Your Own Bank Movement? It is because they made a decision to engage in the process to Be Your Own Bank. I want you to think about the thought process or what it takes to make a decision—it is about you being willing to go against the status quo, and against the norm. But, honestly, what is really the norm? What is the percentage of the population who understand systematically how to generate and create wealth? So, when you think about the decision you have made, you did not just make a decision to engage in the BYOB Movement; you made a decision to take ownership of your personal life.

In most cases, most individuals, when they look at where they are, have allowed other people to create their narrative and create their roles as well as how much time they deserve to spend with their family, and how much revenue they deserve to bring home to that place where they reside. Then we allow, without thinking through the process, accepting the value of what people believe about us. We internalize that and we just accept living a life of mediocrity.

Because of the mere fact that you as a leader have decided to make a decision to create and develop a mindset to learn a skillset and, most importantly, to be responsible for the true financial legacy for you and your family, we salute and applaud each and every one of you.

We launched this initiative on 11 January, 2018, but it came up under the criticism that we did not know all the information necessary to execute. What we did know is that because I personally had a long-standing relationship with my financial institution, I did not need to know everything to be able to begin to share the information with people that I felt needed to know it. That was point Number One. Point Number One for you is understanding the reason why you accepted the challenge to Be Your Own Bank. All the innovators that have accepted the challenge are extra ordinary people when it comes to making decisions and being pertinent.

What I want you to internalize is that you are the CEO of your life. When looking at any Fortune 500 company or any successful business, realize that it started with the individual who saw something and made a decision based on their circumstance. So, when you're looking at you, the individual being the CEO of your life and making a decision to be able to move forward, find the shortest path to reaching that financial destiny which you feel you deserve and, most importantly, that you are willing to say, "You know what? I'm drawing a line in the sand today, and I'm going to do everything within my capabilities. I'm going to do anything from this standpoint, and I'm going to do what's required. Then I'm going to do what's necessary because every top CEO on the planet starts at the same place. They all start with the conversations they have with themselves." So, when you look at some of the great business minds on the planet, they are no different than you.

This journey begins with you having that conversation with yourself, understanding that if you're not going to do it, it won't get done. Understanding when you look at some of the names that we may be familiar with, that you can get there too. When I look at, and think about the name JP Morgan, when I think about the name Rockefeller, when I think about Vanderbilt, I know these individuals had the same thing that you and I have. They had the intellect; they had the belief in themselves, and they did not allow anyone else, externally, to determine that for them.

So, internally, as you have accepted the Be Your Own Bank Challenge within the BYOB movement, I want to share with you some of the elements of the framework that successful entrepreneurs understand. This is what we call the Four Stages of Learning. It doesn't matter your tenure; it doesn't matter how long you've been with this process or if you are just beginning the process. I want to help you understand systematically the process of becoming a successful CEO and, most importantly, the CEO of your life. We all start at the same place.

* * *

The first of the Four Stages of Learning is what we call Unconscious Incompetence. That simply means that we don't know that we don't know. So often we've come up in environments or familiar structures (you know our lineage) and because of that environment, there are things that we just don't know that we don't know. For example, many of you probably didn't recognize that the foreign exchange market existed and the manner in which it has existed, and because you really weren't aware of it, you didn't know about it. So, you didn't know that you didn't know. Additionally, you probably did not know that you could participate, learn this skill, and become your own bank. Why is it important that I am addressing this? So when you end up sharing this information with people who are not familiar with it, you cannot allow the fact that they don't know that they don't know alter or determine the viability of what you are embarking upon and allow that to be a deterrent. It doesn't matter where the information comes from. I'm helping you understand. It could be someone that you hold dear to yourself. It could be a parent; it could be your professor, or it could really be anyone. So, unconscious incompetence should not lead you to believe that the information does not exist and is not viable. That's the first position as a CEO and the architect of your life; that's where you are right now.

The second stage of learning is what we call Conscious Incompetence where you know that you didn't know. When you become aware of it, you are beginning to understand that there's a different set of information that now is allowing you to take ownership of your life and create the right habits and the right behaviors to get the right outcomes. So that's the second stage or what we call conscious incompetence.

At this stage you are now aware, so you have taken the time to dive into your newfound understanding and education of this new language. This is a new concept, and I want you to understand not to become overwhelmed. You may get frustrated. It's just a part of the stages of learning; it's ok. Even if you've been doing this for six months or 12 months, or even for only two weeks or three days, it is still the process of learning. So what, it's okay. It's okay because you're beginning to write your story, and thus beginning your awaking to your conscious competence, where you now realize you have begun to understand. It now becomes an exercise that you execute, because now you're creating the right habits. So what does this mean? It is designed to get you to think differently, so that you can leave the past way of thinking behind.

Now you're at that place to transition to stage three of learning, Conscience Competence. This is where you begin to identify where you are and begin to intentionally act accordingly. So how do we accomplish this? We have systems in place to create the results. Now that you're aware that you are the CEO and the architect of your whole life, you begin to work on the habits to bring you to a level of efficiency that's going to create those desired outcomes from a trading perspective as well as from an opportunity to share the information perspective. When you have great information, you generally want to share that information with the people within your sphere of influence.

The fourth stage of learning is called Unconscious Competence when you simply do what you know. Now, most of us, when we become familiar with things, we've become familiar with processes. Some of you have been in your workplaces 2 years, 10 years, 20 years, or whatever the case may be. It's what we call being on autopilot. That's when you just simply do what you know. That's the purpose of plugging in,and that's the premise of staying plugged in. I can assure you, no matter what you're doing in life, when you have mastered what we call mastering the mundane, then you now have the opportunity to maximize and get the earning benefit of true wealth.

Now that you know the four stages of learning, I need you to identify where you are right now. Stage number one is unconscious incompetence when you don't know that, you don't know; that's okay. Start there and identify it. Second is conscious incompetence, now that you know, you're aware of it. So you begin to take the right actions in order to get the right results. And this may be the most difficult transition for a lot of us. A lot of us have been programmed to believe that, our true goal is to accumulate, and acquire that collegiate experience, and that collegiate degree so we can work a job for 20 - 30+ years.

This process is what you may be most accustomed to and most familiar with, but if you look at the grand scheme of things, and if you're honest with yourself, you have to question why individuals get different results? It's because of what they've been exposed to. When you get better information and you execute, this is stage three, conscious competence when you exercise that liberty of taking advantage of systems designed to create wealth. You will ultimately transition into stage four of unconscious competence where you just do what you know. At some point you're going to be able to lead and guide masses of people to a new thought process and to a new level of self-appreciation. That's why as the CEO and the architect of your life, you have to be responsible for acknowledging where you are and then, most importantly, being ready to follow effective processes to get to the next place.

These are the Four Stages of Learning. This is where you are. This is the purpose of leadership. This is the purpose of understanding and what we've been able to do systematically within the BYOB Movement.

* * *

I want you to understand the culture of the BYOB Movement, and the culture of what we are creating to reach and financially educate and empower one million families. Understand the power of your yes. Because of your yes, lives will be changed and families will be touched. Because of my yes, a vision has unfolded. I have a background in investment banking. I have had the fortunate opportunity be a part of a well-known company's IPO, or Initial Public Opportunity. This is why I have been afforded the opportunity to be the face of the same type of propriety tool that the big banks of the world use and this is why the movement has adopted the name Be Your Own Bank. You have the opportunity to participate in a market that your banks and financial institutions have been participating in with your money. You have the same opportunity. This is the environment and the community that we've been able to create.

It does not matter if you were just informed about the foreign exchange market today or last week, you do not have to know everything involved with the training because you have someone who can do that for you. He has been studying this information that has been hidden in plain sight. He is Dr. Craig Bythewood who has specialized in education over the past 26 plus years. He is the first African American to receive his PhD in finance and economics from the University of Florida and at that time was the 11th in the country. He has been a chief financial officer, educator and consultant. You can get excited about knowing the CEO of your operation, about knowing that you have someone who can excel in that department, and it's okay that you don't know the information yet because now you have someone you can learn from who is willing to pour into you.

You have Tasha M Dyer, creator of the BYOB Cashout strategy and WomenTEACH4x Movement. She is a retired major of the United States Army. She has an MBA and is a licensed financial advisor. She is also coaching and teaching individuals around the world. More importantly, both of these experts have a servant heart, and they naturally and organically want to mentor you and all they come in contact with.

It is important for you to understand how to utilize this message and the validity of it. You'll get results because of what we've begun doing behind the scenes and knowing the vision has now unfolded. You now have the opportunity to impact the entire landscape and foundation of educating and impacting one million families. You're shaping the culture of your family, the culture of your community, and the culture of generations to come.

I'm grateful that you are part of allowing this vision to manifest. So what am I saying? I've talked to you about the four stages of learning. I've already shared with you the impact that you're having. It's never about an individual. It's all about us collectively as we all individually celebrate the parts that bring it all together, the middle members. It's one body, of different functionality but of equal importance and equal value. That's the environment. That's what the BYOB challenge is all about. It's okay if you are just being exposed to the BYOB Movement and the foreign exchange market. You're in that first stage of learning. You don't know that you don't know. But if you keep reading and make the decision to Be Your Own Bank you will inevitably begin to get the results and outcome you desire.

There is greatness in each and every one of you. There's absolutely no way that you would be here out of all the people on the planet, particularly here in the United States, over 320 million, unless you now have the opportunity to be a part of something that's going to have an impact globally. The fact is that you are having an impact, even though you did not even realize it; it was sitting around you making the decision and deciding, "Do you know what? I deserve more. My family deserves more, and I'm willing to do something different in order to get a different result."

Chapter 4

Plan Your Life

Are you ready to get started? We're your coaches, we're your mentors, but, most importantly, we're individuals who want to see you win and win in the most unique way possible. The essence of your being the chief executive officer of your life is really why this book and its message are so significant. It's centered on you as an individual and, most importantly, the habits that you and I have. What you are about to experience is different.

Think about your personal life and where you are financially. Think about the things that you've done. No matter how long you've been in the workforce, no matter how long you've been an entrepreneur, no matter how long you've been where you are, you can completely agree that you are where you are because of the habits that you've participated in every single day.

We want to begin by making sure that we calibrate and continue to recalibrate the habits that are producing the results you have desired and which have led you and I to the place of financial prosperity where we currently are. You have to continue to create habits to lead you towards more wealth.

So, just think about your life. Let's begin to plan your life over a 30 day period at the beginning of the month. If your calendar has not been planned out for the upcoming month, then you need to operate a little bit differently in order to get different results. If you're not planning your life, I can assure you that someone else is planning your life for you. Someone else is planning your income because you've allowed them the opportunity to dictate the narrative and your household is receiving the efforts that you participate in on a day-to-day basis.

This is about leadership. You are the chief executive officer of your life. You're an individual who had made a conscious decision that you are personally taking ownership of your life. Whether you realize it or recognize it or not, you are the chief executive officer of your own life, so the results that you have been getting are a result of your economic understanding and your economic position.

To plan your life, you must first take ownership of that and say, "Why am I getting the results that I'm getting? I am the reason why I'm gaining or not gaining when it comes to my economic understanding and my economic viability." That's the first step in becoming the chief executive officer of your own life, taking ownership.

Most of us have been led to believe that the income we are receiving, whatever source it may be coming from, is based on what people will allow us to obtain. That is absolutely not true! I'm going to give you tremendous pushback on that and say that when you make up in your mind to be great, you will be great. When you make up in your mind to be wealthy, you will be wealthy. Now, what do you have to do? You have to focus on your IPAs, "Income Producing Activities." This is the magic formula that most people think is a vast array of things. However, I'm going to remind you that no matter who you are, we are all simply the product of the habits we have produced.

Those habits are indicative to your financial viability. What do I mean by this? Well, it starts with this. You took the initiative to begin your journey to accept the Be Your Own Bank Challenge, saying yes to beginning this journey, to learning the skillset of trading in the financial markets. It's a mindset. It's a process. It's a habit of plugging into the Be Your Own Bank (BYOB) system.

Habits and lifestyles are things that separate the best from the rest, your level of execution and why you would say that other individuals seemingly have advantages or not. No, it's not that they have an advantage; it's all in the application and the habits. As you self assess yourself over the past six months, what habits have you been consistently entangled in that have led you to where you are right now? Let that sink in for a second. Some of you may find that to be a sobering thought, but for some of us who understand where we're headed, it's something to build upon. Planning your life includes making the transition to transform yourself while shifting the habits that have led you to where you are. If you are satisfied where you are right now, then I'm going to assert to you that you're not working hard enough, and if you are satisfied where you are based on the work you have produced, then I'm going to assert to you again that you're not working hard enough because you and I should always be evolving, and we should always be excelling. We should always be pushing ourselves to be the best because there is no one who subdues our ability to expand other than ourselves.

When looking at yourself right now, how do you evaluate yourself? You need the ability to operate in complete and total excellence every single moment, every single day. How are you facilitating right now? What are you doing differently today, this moment, than you did 24 hours ago, than you did 15 minutes ago? When you look at yourself, evaluate yourself from the understanding that you and I are the sum total of our habits, our thoughts, and of what we do.

The majority of the individuals who say that they're in pursuit of financial gain, and are in pursuit of their dreams and their passions, are actually generally wasting a lot of time. Therefore, as you begin planning your life and your financial endeavors, your activities will either drive you closer to those financial goals or they will drive you further away from them. It's really just that simple. It has been stated that individuals typically spend almost half of their time gossiping. Ask yourself what conversations you are having? Are those conversations leading you closer to your financial goals or are they leading you further away from your financial goal? Another **32%** of your time is generally spent on social interaction that does not produce any financial benefit or any financial income. **26%** of our time is spent sitting around, time that we can't even account for. Then another **24%** of our time is just spent around nonproductivity. In other words, most of our time is non-productive activities that do not enhance our mental capability or mental mindset.

As you plan your life, are you seeing yourself in this equation? The object we should be focused on is our IPAs, our income producing activities, and the habits that we have. Remember, our habits and activities are either leading us closer to our financial goals or further away from our financial goals. When we use our time focused on activities that push us away from our goals, it's an abuse of the time that we've been given. As you begin to transition to holding a more proactive role in planning your life, these non-productive activities must cease in your life. So, when it comes to expanding, when it comes to sharing this information, communicating, and becoming your own bank, you must operate in IPAs.

In order for you to operate in IPAs, you have to internalize a different perception of yourself because you're involved in a $6.6 trillion a day industry, over $11 trillion when crypto currency is added to it. BYOB is going to financially educate and impact 1 million families by 28 March 2021. When we're referencing this financial education and the financial market that is an $11 trillion industry, what would preclude, prevent, or prohibit you from wanting to participate and expose our friends, our neighbors, and our relatives. This information, we know unequivocally is going to put them in a better position financially, simply from an education standpoint. You have the best of both worlds right at your fingertips, but the majority of the time the reluctance to be the foundation of reaching 1 million families is because of what is on the inside of us. So that's why your mind has to be transformed. That's why you have to shift from being too busy to understand being productive. You have to shift your mind and the habits that you have that are either leading you closer to your financial goals or leading you further away. To begin, you have to put a premium on the time that you're utilizing versus time spent on that day-to-day circle, like being on a hamster wheel, doing something over and over that is not leading to financial viability.

I stay excited about the probability, not possibility. The probability is based on a systematic approach and continued, repeated actions. Impressive. So here's what I know to be true. Every individual that you may deem to be financially successful, understood the habits that are needed and they recreated them. Secondly, they understood that every hour that they had, they had the opportunity to equate that to income producing activities. It is going to take some work over a period of time. You're going to be able to obtain those financial goals, but if you're not putting the work in, it's never going to come. Subsequently, if you're not taking ownership and responsibility for your own life, even if you're in the workforce, then that individual who you're beholden to has the right to determine how much they want to offer you or pay you, and if you want to settle for that, then so be it. But what we're doing, what we're creating, is looking to infuse those individuals who realize that they deserve the best and they're willing to pay the price. They're willing to put the work in with the correct behaviors to correct activities, to develop correct habits every single day that's leading them closer to their financial destiny.

You begin your journey by first accepting the challenge to be your own bank. That is first making the decision that you are ready to plan your life and make the mental shift to transform your financial paradigm. No one should have to encourage you or entice you to do that. You should be willing to take ownership of your own life and then help the people with whom you've been called to share this information. You are going to be able to speak intelligently, boldly, and competently about the system. During this transition, you'll go from busy to productive. It all starts with you on the inside of your mind, on the inside of your heart, and with your willingness to throw your hat in the ring and say, "You know what? I'm worth it. I believe it. I need it, and I am pursuing it!" Yes, those are the affirmations. Those are the declarations. That's the focal point. That's the energy of operating in a perpetual excellence that is going to drive and create the right environment and atmosphere and energy that's going to allow you to be the bridge. That's actually allowing individuals who've been in a state of demise by their financial misunderstanding to come across you, because you've laid a firm foundation. It happens because you've made a decision to say, "You know what? I owe it to my family. I owe it to my community to endure this process that we can all be recipients of this wonderful information through our BYOB Challenge and our BYOB Movement!"

* * *

You want to begin with these seven points to your financial freedom that will help you to begin to think positively about money and help you with this mental transition. There's been a lot of miss-teaching regarding money. Here's what you need to understand: Money is a tool and so many of us are fearful because we've been misled, mis-taught and mis-educated. People have put out these innuendos and said that money changes people. No, money only enhances the person that you already are. So, if you are a person of no integrity, no character, in other words, if you are a jerk now, then you will be an even bigger jerk with money unless you take the time to go through a transformation from the inside out.

The first point is for you to think positively about money because your relationship with and your thought processes on how you view money are tied to an emotion. If that emotion is a negative emotion, then you will allow every obstacle that comes up to prevent you from keeping your promise to yourself when you accepted the challenge to be your own bank. So, you have to reengage and reshape your thought process and address the question, "How do you think about money? Secondly, you've got to rewrite your financial goals for your financial freedom. How often are you writing down the purpose of why you desire to have financial freedom? It's not really the money; it's the things that money represents, the intangibles. If you are a person that is going to do good, you're going to do good. But it's tied into what you visualize, what you've written down because that's your purpose. What have you written down about your financial goals? Why is it a necessity for you to stay with the process? You have to see money and think positively about understanding the purpose of the money and when the purpose of the money is tied to the right activities and the right behaviors. Then the universe will readily avail opportunities for you, and you will attract individuals with the same energy that you're producing.

Number three is to plan every day in advance. Planning allows you to create habits. What habits do you have on a day-to-day basis regarding the purpose of your pursuing your goal of becoming your own bank? Every single day ask yourself what you are doing that's leading you closer to the end goal or if your activities are moving you further away?

Number four is the principle of concentration. We have to find ourselves in a place where we're no longer distracted by everything and making sure that when someone distracts us we stay focused. Our agenda must get accomplished and not theirs. Are you willing to concentrate for the next 12 months? Are you willing to stay focused for the next 18 months? Are you willing to stay focused for the next 24 months to ultimately achieve that financial viability that you'd been looking for? It behooves me and makes me often wonder why people will stay focused and concentrated for 20 to 30 years for something they know at the end of the road is never going to produce the lifestyle or the income that they deserve. Ask yourself, why would you compromise? Stay focused.

Number five is to invest in yourself. That means you have to blow a barge in your mind. Be transformed by the renewing your mind. Take ownership of your own narrative. This means you have to spend time in that space of personal development. The more you work on yourself, the bigger your business will grow. That's the purpose of becoming the chief executive officer of your own life. The more you work on yourself, the more you enhance yourself, which is your personal development. Where do you start? An alarming statistic is that the average person spends 500 hours a year in their automobile, so your automobile should become your lab. Anything that you can do to drive you closer to the behavior of achieving your financial goals should be a part of your investing in yourself. So, what are you doing every single day? What does your day look like? What is shaping your habits?

Number six is self-examination. We want you to first understand that there's greatness housed within you. There are two questions that you should be asking. Start with the understanding that if you ask the right questions, you're going to always get the right answer. So the first question you should be asking yourself every single day is, "What did I do right?" So often we've been focused on what we did wrong, but if you rephrase that, you'll shift your focus and get a different response. The second question is, "What would I do differently next time to increase my viability to increase my awareness?" So, these are the two questions. Ask the right questions to get the right answers.

Number seven is be generous. Be generous, and it shall be given to you. Pressed down, and shaken together, shall men give unto your bosom. I get such joy and pleasure in being able to freely give information that has enhanced my life. More people will be attracted as well, because there's no room for selfish ambition or games. Remember that one million families will be financially educated and impacted through your voice, through your actions, through your belief, and through your commitment. You've been called, out of all the multiple people on the planet. You've been given the assignment to stay the course, to stay focused, and to stay purposed in creating legacy wealth. It all starts with you being the chief executive office over your life. It all starts with your governing yourself accordingly, creating the right environment, and recalibrating and recreating habits that have not produced the expected outcomes.

I'm completely persuaded that this culture we're creating is the best environment for both those who've had no success, and those who've had vast success. This philosophy is designed for all people to be plugged into the BYOB Movement, because it's really about servanthood, improving lives, and transforming communities.

Chapter 5

CEO of Your Life

We want to make sure that the importance of creating the right behaviors and the right purpose is understood. As you become the Chief Executive Officer (CEO), it is important you take time to create the proper perspective and understanding. I want you to look at this information from two vantage points.

I want you to look at it from a business aspect, and then I want you to also, most importantly, look at it from a personal standpoint. You've embarked upon a journey where you have entered a space of understanding the financial markets, learning terminology and comprehending a language that will shift your financial paradigm.

Most of the time, when we think about leadership, it is generally focused on the title versus the activity, the functionality, and the understanding of being able to clearly define our roles. We always associate the word CEO from a business standpoint. From this perspective, it is astonishing to look at the life of someone who has bestowed upon themselves the aspect of chief executive officer, of leading a company or organization whose business will thrive based on the daily functionality of how well that chief executive officer leads his or her own personal life.

I want what you to always focus on your being a chief executive officer of your life. As CEO, the first thing that needs to happen is for you to embrace the phrase and begin to look at it from a personal viewpoint. CEOs create, understand, disseminate information, and communicate effectively. So there two questions that you always want to ask yourself at the end of the day. How well did you lead yourself? What did you do today that would make you want to follow you?

Imagine this, as you look at the space we operate in. We're looking at the foreign exchange market, and we have multiple charts; the daily chart, the four-hour chart, and the minute chart are a few of them. In the market, we can describe or ascertain what's going on with the market based on looking to the left. So for the big picture, we look at that daily chart, and we see the overall movement of what's happening on the chart. Then for us to get a more detailed report, we look to the left to the four-hour chart. Then we go back to the minute time frame to get a more accurate point. Apply this same concept to your life. Think about it, if you are the CEO of your own life, the activities of the charts would also align with what we would do in our lives. So, how well are you leading yourself on a day-to-day basis? When you look at your daily activity and then go back to timeframes of your life, what are you doing on a minute-to-minute basis? The magnificent thing about being the chief executive officer of your life is no matter what actions you're taking—good, bad or indifferent—it is going to be indicative of the big picture of your life. No matter where you are in your personal relationships and your business relationships, consider how well you are executing? Own it on that minute chart because that's the one that you will need to master to become a successful chief executive officer of your life. It is all designed around IPAs, income producing activities. When you think about you being the CEO of your life, consider the results you've achieved in your life. When you do so, you will continue to get results based on your IPAs, your income producing activities. Some activities may vary because there is a unique difference in us all, but when you look at the household names of those fortune 100 companies that we all consider to be great companies, realize that they have been led by individuals who have collectively created an atmosphere to obtain results. So how often are we avid leaders when it comes to our own personal lives? Are we more focused on the activity? Are we really focused on the results that will be produced?

Think about the great names of the world, such as the Warren Buffets and Bill Gates, who have perfected being the CEO of their own personal lives. It just spills over to their business activity. Let's put some context to the word chief. A chief is an executive or leader of people. But the question that I always want to make sure we are operating in is, "Are you leading yourself?" See, leadership starts with you. How well do you lead yourself? And if you're leading yourself properly, the question you then have to ask yourself is, "What did I do today that would make me want to follow me?" Let that sink in for a second. If you can say that you'd follow yourself because now you're walking into success, that's the beginning of you being able to consider yourself a leader. But no one will ever follow you until you can govern yourself. Hold yourself accountable to the steady motto: We have good, we have better, we have best, and then we have excellent. So as the chief executive officer of your own life, do only things that you want to ascribe to as excellent because you've been created to operate in greatness. You've been created to have dominion. That means you have the authority to bring about things and to have a constant purposed outcome of excellence, if you speak and declare it over yourself.

Are you in tune with the outcomes? The wonderful thing about people and about the universe is that you and I have the same amount of time that's allocated to everyone. So you often wonder why individuals are always getting different results. It's because they have embraced an understanding. They've made the conscious decision to be the chief executive officer of themselves first and foremost. It all begins with you leading your life.

This begins with creating a vision for your life and being able to execute and articulate it. Let's look at the life of Jeff Bezos, CEO of Amazon. He had an idea to allow people to get books without having to go to a bookstore. That was the initial thought process and then it became so successful, he began to scale it up because he understood profit centers and distribution. By performing this scale up, now you can literally get anything and everything from an online purchase experience with his company. As a result he became the wealthiest person in the world because he understood how to govern his own personal life on a day-to-day basis. The CEO is an individual who is always decisive, adaptable, and forward thinking.

Your mindset is how everything begins. Poor people live day-by-day, broke people live month-by-month, Rich people live year-by-year, and wealthy people live decade-by-decade. Everything that you and I do has to be premeditated. In other words, you have to be responsible for your own programming or else you will adapt to and embrace someone else's programming for your outcome. The mind of a CEO is an individual who is decisive in the thought process. CEOs are able to make decisions, good, bad, or indifferent. If you look at your life and the people that are around you and the people you have influence over that are around you, you can instantly expect someone to be successful or not based on their ability to make a decision. When it comes to exposing people to this information, I do not have any attachment to a person saying yes or no. However, I am going to ensure that they make the decision. If they don't make a decision, then I realize, as CEO, that this is not the individual that I need to continue telling my story to.

So, we must stay focused on the mind of a CEO and their responsibilities. A CEO is responsible for creating culture. Culture represents the customs and arts, social institution, and achievements of a particular organization. So what culture are you creating as the CEO of your life? Have you created a culture of being entertained by watching programs? Listen to the word programs that are designed to keep you income-restricted. What are those programs? What programs are you watching? If you're going to entertain yourself, what programs are you endowed with that's keeping you in a place of income restriction. Remember, all of us have the same amount of time, the same 168 hours a week. CEOs are always controlling their time based on the outcomes that they're looking to produce and the results. Our activities are leading us toward or away from our financial goals.

The culture that we are creating is a culture of success. Samuel Truett Cathy is the CEO of one of the most lucrative restaurant chains in the world. If you're not familiar with who S. Truett Cathy is, he is the CEO of Chick-fil-A. Chick-fil-A is completely successful because they have established a culture of excellence. No matter how many times I go to Chick-fil-A drive thru they're going to make sure my order is correct and that I have a pleasant experience. So when you look at you as the CEO of your life, what culture have you created for yourself? What can people anticipate when they have an encounter with you? Can they count on you when you say you're going to do something; have you created that culture? Have you held yourself to a higher standard of excellence? Have you moved from being good to better, to great, to excellent? What culture are you creating? Your desire has to be to create a culture of success.

Success is about an infrastructure that can be carried out in your absence. It is not respective of a person or personality, but it's the system that allows you to experience perpetual greatness. It's all about the system and the understanding of what we are here for. It is about what we are designed and purposed to do, who we are. It is about our system, our mission, and our vision. It is about the mindset and culture that you want to be responsible for creating as you develop and establish profit centers and distribution channels around the world.

I want you to understand what we call the four E's. The first E is to equip you with the right information. Our entire purpose with the first E is that we are here to equip you with the right information so that you can execute in excellence. The second E is to <u>empower</u> you so that you can reproduce after your own kind. We all have a responsibility to reproduce and grow. Number three is to <u>expand</u> your mind. Be transformed by the renewing of your mind as you begin to operate and think like a CEO. That's the foundation of our movement of BYOB. Think like a bank. Now we need to help you think like a CEO, like a chief executive officer of your own life. Lastly, we are here to <u>exist</u> because the purpose of leadership is to grow greater than ourselves. Greater works shall you do. So from a systematic standpoint, I expect, I anticipate, I believe if we are really successful that over the next 90 days, you will begin to evolve and you will begin enlarging your territory. You should be expanding your sphere of influence because you are now operating like a chief executive officer. That's how the movement always stays alive. The vision is to financially educate one million households. So the question is as the chief executive officer, how many of those one million families that we are going to financially educate will you be responsible for creating?

That is the vision. That is the purpose. The message is very clear. How many individuals do you feel you know that we would love to or need to be exposed to this information? There are a lot of words that you'll have to contend with when it comes to telling our story and accomplishing this objective. You may be familiar with a word called objections. These are reasons that people object or believe that they do not want to be a part of growing and learning or changing of their lives. However, I've come to discover that a lot of the objections we anticipate receiving from individuals are really objections that we have in our own minds. As

CEOs, we have to first think and extract those objections out of our own mind because, if they are in us, we project them onto other individuals. If we are operating in that energy of doubt, fear and unbelief, we are projecting that as well.

Some of the words that we have to contend with are the words cost, price, and value. First, I want you to invert your thought process and think from a perspective of a business owner, from a chief executive officer's perspective. The word cost sometimes triggers emotions, and we realize that people often focus on the wrong side of the equation, but, because you now understand this as a chief executive officer, it is going to help you communicate your message in a story that will get you the proper outcome. So, where is the cost? Cost is what it takes to produce a service, the amount that you spend to bring it to the market. As a chief executive officer of your life, the cost to you is changing your paradigm to learning a new skillset. That's the cost! That's the price of getting different outcomes. The cost to you right now is being inconvenienced. Even if you're working full time, the cost to you is making sure you allocate that extra hour, hour and a half, to be uncomfortable. That simply means that paying the cost now, 12 months from now you can gain the life that you've dreamed about. This means from nine to five you're doing what you have to do to pay your bills, but from six to ten you're doing what's necessary to create the lifestyle that you desire, that you want to have. That means it's costing you some TV time. That means those programs that are not yielding income or revenue need to be eliminated from your existence at this present time to be replaced with those that are productive. Now you can excel and change your financial understanding and financial legacy. That's what the cost is. The price is the financial reward that you receive from investing in yourself. That's the reward! You've taken the time to disrupt your life. You've taken your time to make sure that you plug into the BYOB system. The price is that now you're able to grasp concepts; you're getting different outcomes. You are beginning to learn the trade, the BYOB Cashout strategy. You're now in a position to reap the reward of what the cost was for you to change your habits. Lastly, value is what you believe you receive based on your life of inconvenience. You already know, based on where you are right now, the things that you did not know, no matter how long you've been in this process. You didn't know what the foreign exchange market was. You didn't know what a candle was. You didn't know what a pullback was, so that's the value that you can present to those individuals that you influence because you know it has worth to that individual because you realize how much and where you would be had you been exposed to the information five years ago, 10 years ago, or 15 years ago. Can you imagine how different your financial paradigm would be? You are participating in a market that is comprised of $6.6 trillion a day. Think about how different your family's history would be? Can you imagine the value of deciding to embrace personal development? Can you imagine had you had the understanding of what you're gaining right now, how different your personal life would be? But here's the wonderful caveat. We have children, grandchildren, nieces, and nephews. Can you imagine? Because you've made a decision to operate and be the chief executive officer of your life, there is a great value to generations to come because of the decision you're making right now. It reminds me of Job in the Bible when he is told,

"...your latter shall be greater." At the end of Job, his latter was greater than the beginning. So no matter where you are right now, as a chief executive officer of your life, wherever you are, you can be assured that because you have had a paradigm shift, because you have had a transformation on the inside, the value that you will bring to your community, the value that you bring to your family, the value that you bring into your place of worship and fellowship, you now can write your own story because you made a conscious decision to be the chief executive officer of your life. You made a constant decision to understand and embrace a culture of success. You made a constant decision to say, "You know what? I'm no longer settling for a life of mediocrity. I'm going to operate and be the chief executive officer of my daily functionality, my daily life, which ultimately will lead to my creating profit centers and distribution channels literally around the world."

Chapter 6

Emotional Intelligence Leads to Financial Profitability

To ensure that you have the proper understanding of how to create distribution centers across the globe, it all starts with creating the right habits. You must participate in your personal development and growth. When it comes to creating and building a successful business, the key to being successful is really in understanding how to govern yourself. The more you work on yourself, the bigger your business will be become. As always, we're speaking from a leadership perspective, from a mind of a CEO, chief executive officer. The mindset that ensures longevity and perpetual growth is always going to be centered on how you as the individual are leading yourself on a day to day basis.

I want to reiterate the questions that you must ask yourself on a day-to-day basis: What did I do today that would make someone want to follow me? Would I follow me based on what I've done over the last seven days pertaining to building my financial empire? Consider this. Did you put the required time in to improve your trading skills? Did you put the required time in to messaging that makes people want to follow? So those are questions that you always have to ask yourself, and you should be able to, on a day-to-day basis, check those boxes in the affirmative because we're always speaking about talking and walking in excellence. Are you being excellent every single day, or are you still focused on being mediocre and doing just barely enough to get by? That's the main question that you always want to be able to answer in the affirmative if you're looking to be that successful CEO that you envision yourself being. Whether you're there or not, the actuality or the manifestation of it does not come to fruition until you envision it yourself. So, what are we talking about when we speak about being a chief executive officer? Often we're talking about leading the masses, but you begin to lead the masses by leading yourself every single day. Are you comfortable with the outcomes when it comes to your economic brevity and your economic viability on a day-to-day basis? If you look at the month you're about to close and the month you closed last month, what is different mentally about you at this very moment, at this very second and at this very millisecond? Our desire and our hope is that you mentally are improving and everything that is happening on the inside, you are now able to articulate from a verbal perspective. I stay excited about your success, and where you're going as CEOs of your own personal life. Now, as you begin to create and understand that particular dynamic, you now begin to attract other likeminded individuals because you have become a magnet. What we attract is based on what our thought processes are and the energy that we are consistently walking in.

That's why every single moment, you have to be premeditated regarding your financial outcomes. You have to be premeditated in rehearsing your life in order to create a different dynamic. How do you become the magnet to financial mogul that you know exists? We are in this environment where income is readily available, and, as you begin to understand the concepts of trading, as you begin to understand the concepts of sharing this information, the thing that is going to allow you to remain profitable is how consistent you are and understanding who you are. When you look at the great minds and the great CEOs in the world, there are a couple of things that I want to bring to the forefront to influence your thoughts moving forward as you continually embark or the next phase of your financial life. Now, pause for a second and remind yourself of this. Have you ever heard the phraseology that attitude is everything? Let that sink in for a second! Attitude is everything. You could have two individuals who can be experiencing the same type of upheaval in their life. They could come out of the same household. They could be siblings, from an environment that statistically isn't favorable for the outcomes. However, you have two individuals who've not been given the best of opportunities, the best of chances, and yet they have two different outcomes. Why? Because attitude is everything! I want to help you expand on that concept, and I want to challenge your thought processes. Ask yourself the question, "Why is it so often people have dreams and desires, and they either achieve them or they don't?" One of the labels that society holds on to about achieving those dreams is your IQ. You've heard it. You have to be intelligent, you have to be smart, and you have to get good grades. Really, it's just another thought process. You experienced people that may not necessarily be as smart as you based on the scores that they received, but they handle situations and circumstances in completely and totally different ways. In order to be an effective CEO, you have to evolve into a higher level of what we call emotional intelligence. Emotional intelligence and the individuals who eclipse this threshold of emotional intelligence will always be your top income producers, will always be your top people who lead causes because they've been able to tap into a place that most people choose not to venture into. Consider the verse of scripture that says, "...be angry, but sin not." What does that mean? It means the emotion is real. The anger is real. But how often do you and I fail to accomplish those things because we allow our reaction to supersede our logical processing of data and information, which is the distinct difference between being emotionally intelligent and emotionally flawed.

So, when you look at how you were able to overcome things that happened in your past that were not favorable, will it all be housed in how emotionally mature you are? Your emotional maturity is going to be the variable that differentiates whether you are successfully moving forward, or if you are remaining stagnant and stifled based on your own perception of yourself. The purpose here is to reintroduce you to yourself and help you to appreciate the greatness that is housed in your mental state. I just want to bring you to a place where you're now able to overcome any level of lack of emotional intelligence so that you can supersede the outcomes that you, thus far, have been able to produce when it comes to your financial viability.

We must always be thinking about walking and talking, about improving, operating and becoming excellent. So here are some of the things that are manifest when you have not become emotionally mature. Some of the emotions that we experience when it comes to doing those things that we know we should be doing mentally because we have the mental capacity to do so, the mental understanding; however, we allow our emotions, our reaction, to lead us, not how we should respond to a particular situation. Remember, your response takes logical processing and allows your brain to supersede the initial emotion and lead you to a place of moving forward or recording.

Consider how you tend to react to some situations that are always going to be based on your emotional override. Case in point, if you attempt to stick your finger in your eye, your reaction would be to blink or close your eyes. However, if you're playing athletic sports and you're in an environment where there are consistent opportunities for your eye to be damaged, what's the response? The response would be for you to put on some goggles, some glasses to protect your eye. You would take those steps, rather than close them as that would be detrimental. That's the difference between understanding and having emotional intelligence. These are those things that are part of why you haven't accomplished those things you felt you should have by now. It's all tied to your emotional intelligence. Once again, remember, you can have two individuals from the same household, with the same set of parents, the same challenges, the same circumstances, but depending upon their emotional intelligence, they experience tremendously different outcomes and output.

There are ways to improve your area of emotional intelligence, but you must first identify the indicators that signal you may be operating at the lowest level of your personal emotional intelligence. One indicator that you're operating at your lowest level of emotional intelligence is finding yourself feeling lonely or having loneliness. You find yourself having fear about any and everything. How about frustration? How about guilt? How about bitterness? How about depression? How about instability? How about lethargy? How about disappointment? How about obligation? How about anger? How about feeling like you've failed in everything that you've attempted? How about procrastination? Those are all part of emotional intelligence. Yes, because we all have challenges, we all have obstacles, depending upon our emotional maturity, we all respond to those challenges differently. How do we want to operate? We want to operate in the highest level of emotional intelligence so that when we view those obstacles, they're simply just obstacles, and we allow our cognitive processes and our emotional strength to create outcomes that supersede the current obstacles we face.

Everything is coming from the inside out. Any external circumstances which you are faced with has little to no bearing on keeping you from overcoming that obstacle. So guess what? I, as the emotionally mature individual, realize and understand that it is my responsibility to change my outcomes. Yes, I may be facing tremendous obstacles, but my emotional maturity allows me, number one, to understand having a high level of emotional maturity keeps me in a place of motivation. That means I'm responsible for how I feel. I'm no longer allowing people's responses to dictate my belief in what I'm doing from my family. I'm no longer allowing a person's thoughts of negativity make me doubt my purpose, and I'm moving toward creating financial wealth and sharing this skillset. If you look at any person who has had any level of success, it's because they've arrived at that level of high emotional intelligence. They're focused on the process of creating. They always have peace of mind while things are going awry in the situation they could be facing, but their emotional maturity helps them understand everything that they're facing is short term. They're balanced, and they have self-control. They operate in a place of contentment, and they operate in a place of perpetual desire and appreciation. Where are you right now? If you had to analyze yourself when it comes to your personal emotional maturity, are you operating at a place of high emotional maturity or are you operating in a deficit because you have chosen not to explore every outcome that is favorable? Are you allowing your circumstance to keep you in that place of deficit because you've not improved in your emotional maturity? So, pause and think about it for a moment: The mind of a CEO. Enhancing your emotional intelligence.

When you look at the charts do you see it as an obstacle? Then you have not quite grasped the concept of a trendline, and support and resistance. Does that emotion make you say, "You know what; I'm done with this!" This is an emotion of immaturity, or are you going to say, "You know what; the mother of all learning is repetition. I'm going to stay committed to the BYOB system and study hall. I'm going to ask questions so that I can become empowered. I'm in control of all of my emotions as the CEO. I'm going to do it and follow the process. I've got to stay committed to step by step until I accomplish the task. I'm going to stay focused on the end result and not get trapped in the process because I know if I continue the process, it's going to yield the results, so I'm no longer concerned about how soon it happens, only that it happens."

Why is emotional intelligence very important? First, it's important because it's going to ensure your perpetual success. What happens when you are operating in a place of emotional maturity as a CEO of your own life, and as CEO of your own business? This applies to every aspect of your life because becoming a successful CEO is really about understanding how to cultivate and inspire individuals and how to create proper relationships. That's how you become successful! Understanding relationships, understanding the dynamics of people and being able to understand and identify when someone is lacking in that place of emotional maturity based on their response gives you a competitive advantage. It's creating an environment that's going to be conducive to the outcomes that you desire. Secondly, it allows you to work and operate at your best level because we want the optimal outcomes. We want the optimal results. We want everyone to embrace the thought process, the mindset to operate in excellence every single moment, and if all of us as a collective conscious embrace that thought process, then we're going to always attract people of integrity, people of quality, and have a desire to always evolve into the best of the best. That's the purpose of having a high level of emotional intelligence, and guess what else happens when we operate in a consortium of a collective consciousness? Negative energy and gossip diminish. It disappears because everyone is equally excited to see how big and how vast collectively all of us coming together can move the needle to its highest place. When you get to a place where you are able to execute a trade and you're able to share this opportunity freely and confidently, you'll get excited and know the work that we're all putting in collectively is going to be a benefit to others for years and years to come. That's the purpose of the mind of the CEO and operating in emotional intelligence at its highest level. We're never satisfied with what we did yesterday; we're always looking to improve. We're always looking to expand and create the proper value. Our development is perpetual because of the great minds that we've been able to assemble. As our mantra states, "We're always a student." I'm always seeking out better information to improve myself and ultimately improve what we all are doing collectively. Almost every successful individual on the planet has been able to completely differentiate between their intellectual intelligence and their emotional intelligence. Studies have shown that those individuals who have excelled in their emotional intelligence have created some of the most successful dynasties when it comes to economic environments. So, was it all necessarily about being the smartest person? Probably not. But there are a lot of smart people who don't have the emotional intelligence that coincides with the intellectual capability, and on the opposite side there are some people who may not be necessarily intellectual, but they understand human behavior, they understand emotional intelligence, and they've excelled. This is why a majority of billionaires in America who have not acquired their collegiate degrees understand the psychology of individuals. They have embraced and they have expanded their emotional intelligence and they understand and they have developed great people skills.

Often, you've seen and understood that there are some people who are very intelligent, but they have very little to no emotional intelligence, which makes following them very difficult. The purpose of having emotional intelligence is to make it easy for people to want to follow you. That's how, as the chief executive officer of your life, you become very successful. Would you follow you based on what you've done this day regarding your business empire? Would you follow you based on what you've done over the last seven days? Always challenge yourself. Think about it. Are you willing to give your place of employment more than you're willing to give yourself? If that's not the case, always make sure that you give yourself everything necessary in order for you to move the needle financially. Even if that means it takes extra time, learn the BYOB Challenge, the BYOB System, and remember that the process is the process.

Chapter 7

Banking History & Why BYOB is Important

BYOB. Being your own bank is obviously a philosophy. It's obviously a concept, but I think that sometimes we need to remind ourselves how we got here historically because it puts us in the right perspective to be able to see the changing trends, to see the shifts in the macro-economic market and to be able to prepare ourselves for it. Therefore, in our quest to be your own bank, a very quick history lesson is in order.

Prior to 1933, banks ran every single component of financial transactions. For anything that anybody wanted to do economically or financially, there was only one institution that allowed you to do it and that was the bank. Here's an example. Recently in an academic financial setting, I was talking about the coupon rate, which is simply a fancy way of saying the interest rate that's paid on a bond. If you invest in a bond, the rate that you get on that bond is called a coupon rate. I was explaining to the group the reason why it's called the coupon rate. Prior to 1933, if one invested in a bond, there was no computer network or no certificate mailed to the investor. Bond investors would walk up to the bank and say, "Hey, I just invested such and such amount of money in this bond." The bank would then give the investor a big sheet of coupons and every six months the investor would tear off one of the coupons, walk up to the bank teller, and give them the coupon. They would, in turn, pay the investor an interest payment. So, to this day, even though there aren't physically coupons anymore, we still call it a coupon rate. Pre 1933, all financial transactions were done at a bank. Well, something happened very interestingly in the decade prior to 1933 known as the 1920s or the roaring twenties. A lot of people think that it's called the roaring twenties simply because the car was being built at that time and cars make a roaring sound. But, in reality, the reason why it was called the roaring twenties is because it was the first time in our history that economically we had very strong uptrends.

To truly understand the concept of the 1920s, you really have to go back 30 years before that, back to the 1890s. The 1890s were big because that was the first time that we ever used technology in order to have sustainable business. Prior to 1890, every single industry, every single measure of wealth, every single measure of abundance was agricultural-based. So you basically had land or crops or animals. That was how you gained wealth. However, in 1890 we had these things called steam engines and railroads and other different types of technology.

We called it the industrial revolution. Why was it a revolution? Because it was the first time that we moved away from agriculture and moved into technology for making money. By the time the infrastructure for all of that had been laid, and by the time companies really started doing well based on that, it was the 1920s, and the 1920s roared. They roared economically

Now, I think that there's value here in understanding the way in which supply and demand works. Why is there a value in understanding supply and demand? Well, for one thing, every single trade that we make, every single indicator that we look at in the foreign exchange market is based on supply and demand. Therefore, having an understanding of how supply and demand works puts us in a better position. Also, as we begin to get better and better at our learning platform and educational platform and understanding of how trades work, we're going to have more and more money that we're going to need to manage. So from our buying patterns to our business patterns to when we actually become our own bank and provide capital to individuals that may not have provided capital for in the past, we need to understand supply and demand so we know how to set ourselves up. There are a plethora of reasons why we need to understand supply and demand. Here is a very interesting but consistent fact that happens with managers when there's a very high growth rate. This high growth rate means this company, this firm, this industry, and this economic area starts doing really well. We have record profits, record earnings, and record dividends being paid to investors. So basically when companies are experiencing very high growth, one of the things they do is purchase infrastructure based on the fact that the growth is really high. I was recently packing for a trip to Atlanta for a basketball tournament. My daughter was standing in the closet and she announced, "You need some more gear!" Okay, she's telling me I need some more gear. The same is true for you. As you continue to make more, as you become wealthier, you're going to have to get rid of some older "clothes" and replace them with "newer clothes." So, that's what managers do when companies are doing really well; they begin to build infrastructure based on the increase of demand. So what I'm saying to you is this: This year, I've got huge profits. So what I'm going to do is to purchase additional infrastructure so I can handle the growth and expansion for next year.

The reality is that it will continue to happen and being able to understand it, we put ourselves in a better position to be stronger managers, not only of our households, but of all of our businesses. When this happens, we describe it with an economic term that is referred to as overcapacity. Once things start going well, business leaders don't expect them to go poorly. They expect them to continue to go up. So what managers do is they purchase too much infrastructure based on their anticipation. That demand next year will be as high as it was this year. They assume that growth next year will be as high as it was last year. But guess what happens? Nine times out of 10 the growth is not as high next year and nine times out of 10 the fact that they purchased so much infrastructure based on an expectation of demand exacerbates the problem. So now, there's a manager who has bought all of this infrastructure prepared for high demand, but it never comes. So now the firm, the company, the town, the organization, the industry, guess what they have to do? They have to cut back. Now, what I just explained to you is the macro economic reason why there are business cycles. There are business cycles because of overcapacity. Companies do well, so they buy things based on the expectations they're going to do well again. When they don't do as well and they have bought a lot of infrastructure, now they're going to have to cut back. This is not about us complaining but about understanding what happens so we can empower ourselves to do things better. Understanding that helps you understand that the macroeconomic flow continues. What do you think is the number one expense or the number one cost for companies? Labor, people, human resources, and salary. When people get laid off, it is because of this economic concept called overcapacity. Growth is high. We buy infrastructure based on it also being high next year. It's not, but we have already bought the infrastructure. Now we've got to cut back. Remember, the 1920s were roaring. There were bigger growth rates than investors had ever seen before in the history of the United States stock market. It was huge. So guess what all the companies did, they started investing in infrastructure. As you and I become better and better at doing what we do, we are going to be managing more people than just our household. Understanding information like this allows us to be in a better position to manage our trades, to manage our businesses, and manage all of the infrastructure that we're going to be responsible for in the future. We've already established that we're changing paradigms here. We're not doing this to stay the same. We're doing this to grow and expand, and when we do, we'll be managing processes just like this. So the in the 1920s overcapacity was bigger than normal because the growth was bigger than it normal, and all the companies started buying in preparation that these growth rates would continue. However, a very interesting thing happened.

Remember, I told you that banks handled all financial transactions, so there were two main roles that banks played prior to 1933. Number one, they took deposits and they loaned out money. This was called the commercial banking profit model. They took deposits and then they used the money from the deposits and they made loans. They obviously charged a greater amount on loans than they did for deposits. That's how banks make money. That was their first function. The second function that banks did was that they were responsible for controlling the process for firms raising capital. When companies decided to raise capital, they may decide to issue stock and have individuals invest in their company, or they may decide to issue bonds and have individuals lend them money. But here's a little known fact: we've all heard of bonds, but we may not have recognized that a bond is just a loan. Literally, a company is borrowing money from someone, and they call it a bond. Why is it called a bond? Bonds are in thousand dollar increments, so, if you invest in a bond, you're basically loaning a company $1,000. If you loan $1,000 to a corporation, and the corporation decides not to pay you back, what are you going to do? Of course you're going to sue. Are you aware that the average retainer in the Tampa Bay area is $2,500 to start? So you're going to pay $2,500 for a lawyer to get back a thousand. The government knew that corporations would pretty much have you in a precarious situation, so the company is **bonded** by law to pay you back. That is the reason why it's called a bond. If you know what you're doing, you will always have a job. If you know why you are doing it, you will always be the boss. So basically banks were responsible for helping corporations to raise capital, whether it was through stocks or through bonds. Very interestingly, not only were banks responsible for these two roles, but they also were free to invest in the stocks of companies. This created a pretty incestuous relationship, because the company that's loaning money to companies is also the company that's helping companies raise capital through investors, but it Is also investing in the stocks of these very companies. So with overcapacity in the 1920s and companies starting to do poorly, guess what those companies did? They went to the banks and asked for a loan. Well, banks could easily see that based on the macro economic force of overcapacity and the fact that these companies had purchased way too much infrastructure to handle the decreasing demand for all products, it was obvious that they should not be loaning more money. However, because the banks were invested in the stocks of the companies, they looked the other way, and they loaned the money anyway. So what happened was that the economic downturn became worse. That's why it was called the Great Depression. This occurred near the end of the 1920s and was made greater by this incestuous relationship that banks had with companies. So the federal government stepped in. We're never going to go through that again because this situation was so devastating to our people. I don't know if you've ever talked to anybody who's been through the Great Depression, but, rest assured, they never got over that experience. They don't trust banks. I counseled a Tuskegee airman, and he had $55,000 in cash at his house because he didn't trust banks because he grew up in the Great Depression. The great depression was great, so the federal government said from now on they were nipping this in the bud. So the first thing they came up with in 1933 was a law called the Glass Steagall Act that separated Wall Street from Main Street by offering protection to people who entrust their savings to commercial banks. This law made two major changes to the banking industry. This meant that from now on, banks were not allowed to hold stocks. Second, they took those two functions that banks did, and they separated them out into what is called commercial banking and investment banking. So as of 1933, to protect people from going through any other situation like that, they took commercial banks, made them one entity, and they took investment banks and made them another entity. When I go through this historical underpinning of how this change played out, I like to use as an example that one of the main investment banks back in the day was J. P. Morgan and one of the main banks back in the day was Chemical Bank who eventually became Chase Bank. Aren't they the same company now, displaying the fact that banks found a way to dance around the restriction?

So now these new rules were in place since around 1933. So from 1933 until around the 1990s, we were operating in that way. Have you ever thought about the fact that Citibank has an umbrella company called City Corporation? Have you ever thought about the fact that Chase Bank has an umbrella called Chase Corporation? I can go on and on because what banks did was they became bank holding companies that held the bank. The banks were not allowed to invest in the stock, but the bank holding companies could do this.

Let's look towards the 1920s again. The reason why It was roaring is because of all the high growth, but let me give you a little bit of the infrastructure on WHY the high growth. Some people identified the roaring 1920's with the roaring of the car or the automobile which was big in the 1920s. The automobile was a new technology that pretty much took the country by storm.

One of the effects of macro economic bank markets or macro economic industries is that if one company, one industry, is doing very well, other industries will start doing well as a result. So the auto was doing so well that other entities like the rubber company or the companies that made the tires and the companies that made the machines or steel or different infrastructure that's used to create the auto, all started doing well. However, by the end of the twenties it imploded.

In the 1990s, there was a new technology that came out that was unlike any technology we'd ever seen. It was called the internet. For those of us who were alive in the 1990s, everything was dot-com, dot-com, dot-com. So the same buzz they had about the automobile in the 1920's, we had the same buzz about the internet, and growth rates were significant. I used to do this investment philosophy that I called the Superbowl Halftime Show Investment Philosophy, and I would go around the country teaching this philosophy, and it was very effective. This is what I would do every year during the Superbowl. I would record those companies that were first time advertisers. Superbowl commercials used to cost $1 million per second. The Superbowl commercials had to be first-time halftime Superbowl commercials in order for this philosophy to work. For example, Pepsi had a commercial every year, but the first year Pepsi advertised, it was a huge investment that they were making for themselves. So if you know you're making a huge investment in yourself for the first time, that means you're about to be a part of the incline mentioned before; you're about to be a part of the roar. The commercial philosophy works very well. Remember I started this in the 1990s, and of all the first-time companies that had commercials in the 1990s, there was a year where there were 33 dot com companies that were first time advertisers on the Super-bowl commercials list. Now, that was the only year that the philosophy didn't work because every other year, if they started it, they kept doing it. But the overcapacity in the internet market was so big, there was so much put into dot-com, they over did it. Only 11 of those 33 companies that started returned the next year. And the year after that, only three companies came back. One of them was Amazon. So my point to you is this: the same thing happened in 1990's as what happened in 1920s. Add to this analysis, that in 1999 we passed a new law called the Financial Services Modernization Act. The Financial Services Modernization Act repealed the Glass-Steagall Act which is what they put in place in 1933 to keep banks in check, but in 1999 they repealed it. Remember, as previously noted, they split up the two functions of banking; commercial banks and investment banks were split. Also, I told you that Chemical Bank was a big bank back then that became Chase. I also told you that J. P. Morgan was an investment bank. So this mechanism was stripped apart that could maintain the integrity of the banking system and not be affected by bank runs. A bank run is where everybody starts to become nervous about their money, so they go to the bank and ask to take out their money. You may not realize it, but banks only keep a small fraction of money on site. So, when everybody starts becoming nervous, they all go to the banks at the same time. There wasn't enough money for them to get their deposits, so it made the Great Depression greater.

In the 1920s there was no governmental interaction that was involved to maintain balance. So the depression became great and it became great very quickly. However, in the 1990s we pretty much did the same exact thing we did in the 1920's, but we had parameters in place such as the federal government, the Federal Reserve, and open market operations took place. So now the government and banking world can intervene and make it seem like there's not an issue. So, was the depression great? Yes, but we just didn't call it great. Was there economic downturn? Yes. We just didn't say it. There was an economic downturn and because we kept looking the other way and not really realizing nor admitting that we were in the situation, it wasn't until 2007 that it finally hit the wall.

We have to understand how banks operate if we're going to be our own bank. We have to understand how macroeconomic policies work. We need to understand how we can take what we're doing right now—foreign exchange trading, crypto currency trading, our ability to be able to manage all of the processes that we need to manage economic empowerment—and put ourselves in a position where we understand just how banks operate. Is this about understanding their mistakes and doing something different? Not really, because we are not in control of that. Mostly, this is about understanding the way banks operate and putting ourselves in a position where we are unaffected. This is literally a trip back through the history of banking and looking at how it impacts what's going on right now because literally we are watching the financial institutions transition from paper currency to crypto currency. We're watching major technologies taking place in our society and we can understand how it works. Think about all the individuals from 1922 to the present who had been laid off because all they were doing was looking at that job, having no idea of the macro economic forces that would cause overcapacity and which would cause them to be part of the decisions being made by managers. By us looking at what's going on, by our identifying the way overall industries work, it makes us more powerful from an economic standpoint.

Chapter 8

The Why Behind
The Indices

Crypto currency, represents the new paradigm shift, it is the new frontier. It's important to understand just how significant this evolution is in our financial markets. To understand where we are going, it's important to understand where we've been. Today we hear terms such as Dow Jones Industrial Average, S&P, and the NASDAQ. But let's take a historical trip to understand these indices and how they developed; then you'll understand your front row seat to the evolution of crypto currency that is currently taking place.

The first index was the Dow Jones Industrial Average. The Dow Jones was created when two people formed a venture by the names of Jones and the other's last name was Dow. They decided that the 1890s were a new time. It's a reality that transcended time because 10 years before this we had something called the industrial revolution, which happened because this was the first time we moved from an agricultural-based society to actually having people make money based on technology. We now had things like steam engines, cotton gins, and railroads that we didn't have before. Before that it was all about the horse. The horse was our vehicle and our work horse, and now we actually have these engines and these machines that had people actually producing and making money. This was a revolution! Since it was an industrial revolution, others wanted to benefit from these new technology companies or these new industrial companies operating and share with them.

The Dow Jones Index decided to pick 30 of the largest industrial companies at that time. Now this is significant because in the1850s there was no such thing as an industrial company. Of course, today it's a common theme, but during this time it was actually a revolution and something that had not been seen before. In selecting the top 30 companies, they created a secret index for these companies. As an analogy, think of it as being the GPA of these firms. Why is it secret? Because this is a secret people will pay for! The Dow Jones works like your GPA in school. A GPA is a numerical way of representing a student's academic performance up to a certain point. It tracks and averages all your grades. The Dow Jones does the same thing with the companies.

The Wall Street Journal was one of the first to purchase the Dow Jones industrial average. So by buying it, using it, and presenting it, they were showing credibility. Since then to present day, we are still discussing the Dow Jones. Again, the purpose of the Dow is based on the use of a numerical index that tracks the stocks of the top 30 companies in the US. Why do we care?

We care because we have access to this foreign exchange market. We have access to the crypto-currency market. If we understand the infrastructure, if we understand the background, if we understand the principles and concepts that undergird this, it now makes every trade, every perception, and everything that we see and deal with have more power because we understand where it's coming from. And of course, by understanding this index, we can profit from trading it, in the same manner in which we do forex pairs.

We are not anti-bank, we are just pro- household. We care about this because we know banks have always positioned themselves well. They profit when the market goes up and when the market goes down. We know that banks have always positioned themselves well. They make money when the market goes up and they make money when the market goes down. This is the same position that you have the opportunity to be in as you have accepted the challenge to Be Your Own Bank! We're simply operating off of the movements. All we care about is that it moves. Nobody goes to an amusement park and predicts which way the ride is going to go. You just enjoy the ride. You just enjoy the fact that it's up and it's down. When it's up, it's up, and when it's down, it's down; you get off a safe ride and say that was fun, let's ride it again. That's what we're doing. Let's ride it again. Let's get that first set of 20 pips, and the case of indices, let's get those points. Now, let's do it again, and let's ride again, and let's ride again, and let's ride again. We're so blessed that we have the opportunity to learn about the index, to understand the logic of how the index works. If the Dow Jones goes up, we can profit. If the Dow goes down, we can still profit. And let's go ahead and complete this.

Let's dive a little deeper because the Dow Jones is not the only index that we use to measure success in the United States. As always, whenever someone has a great idea, someone else will come up with a similar idea. We had never heard of Uber before it appeared, but now there's Lyft. The bottom line is when someone comes up with a good idea, somebody else jumps on the bandwagon as well.

Two other gentlemen one last Standard, and the other last name Poors, merged their companies to form what is known as Standard and Poors Corp, otherwise known as S&P. Standard and Poors is collaborated with an index of 500 stocks. Both indexes are looking at the US market, but The Dow Jones looks at 30 companies, and S&P uses 500 companies. One of the principles you learned in statistics is that as you increase the sample size, the reliability of the data doesn't really change that much. So the S& P 500 and the Dow Jones industrial average pretty much show the same thing. If you look at both of them right next to each other, they're moving together. So, it doesn't really matter which one you use, the Dow Jones just came first. GPA was mentioned earlier. The index is the GPA of all of the included companies. Just imagine one as the weighted GPA and the other as the unweighted GPA, but they are both equally important. So, when you hear the market discussed and it's said that the market is up today or the market is down today, they are referencing both of them.

Now you may be thinking, "We need to understand how crypto currency works," and, "We need to understand how foreign exchange works." Correct? But think about it right now. You are your own business. Right now you are an entrepreneur.

Let's make sure we understand the entire picture. I love taking the complexity of markets and breaking them down and making it easy so we all can walk away with the knowledge. You are beginning to operate like a bank. Let me share

with you two things. First, let me share with you the background on why this is important for companies. There are
all kinds of things we can do with the profits that we're going to make collectively. There's value in our understanding
how the process works. If we ever decide we want to create our own company, we want to understand the way raising capital works. When you are a company, when you are
a firm and you decide you want access to capital, you make
a decision, and the decision is called to list, L. I. S. T. You
want to see where you're listing exactly. Let's say you have a
product to sell. You have to sell it somewhere so you could,
on one extreme, sell it from the back of your trunk. On the
other extreme, you could sell it at Neiman Marcus. No matter where you sell your product (there are different places
that you can place your product), there has to be an actual
place. As a firm, when we decide we want to raise capital
we issue stocks. When we decide we want to let people buy
our shares publicly, we decide where it's going to be. That is
called "listing" the stock.

The company has decided to raise capital by issuing
stock. There are two locations where you can "LIST" your
stock. This where investors can find them. The first location is the physical exchange, which is the New York Stock
Exchange and other smaller exchanges. So, if somebody
wants to purchase your stock, they actually have to go to
that exchange and purchase it. The second location is "not
on an exchange". If you decide not to use an exchange, this
market is called Over the Counter (OTC). Over the counter,
historically, simply means that you went to the bank, and
the bank gave you the stock or the bond over the counter.
As stated previously, before 1933 banks controlled all of
the infrastructure and financial markets, meaning if you

wanted to invest in stocks and bonds, there was no computer. You get on your horse and you ride into town, walk into the bank, and say, "I'd like to buy stock," and then they would pass you that stock certificate over the counter. So to this day we still call it over the counter, or OTC. If you go to Yahoo finance right now and you find a stock that's not on exchange, it will say OTC. If it's done on an exchange, it's at one of those exchanges. If it isn't, if it's not on an exchange, then it's over the counter.

We mentioned earlier that the Dow and Jones created this index based on the fact that they saw what was going on technologically. Dow and Jones and their index represented the fact that in the 1890s things were changing in terms of the way in which technology was affecting industry. The same thing happened at the end of the 20th century because of the 1980s and the 1990s, just like during the industrial revolution in the 1800s. In the 90s you had a dot-com revolution or the internet revolution. What started to happen was that there a lot of big firms who were technology companies and wanted to keep their money in Research & Development. These firms decided not to be on an exchange because the cost associated with being listed on the exchange was around $2 million. These companies that were major technology companies in the late 1980s and 1990s decided to keep that money and to be over the counter or to not be on an exchange. Exchanges had the world famous ticker tape system. This was the scrolling mechanism that displayed stock prices. The OTC market was growing, and they wanted or needed identification as well. During this time of growth and expansion is when the OTC market developed a system of how to present their stock prices to the world. This system, which began as a way to compete with the exchange market, was named the National Association of Security Dealers, Automated Quotation System (NASDAQ). People began to realize that these technology companies had their own rate of return patterns and ultimately they also became an index. Thus, the Nasdaq was born.

Why is this important? It's just a little information to increase our knowledge base of how these markets work and the history of the markets because of where we are today. Can you imagine if you were around in the 1890s and you saw an entire industry being born and then you were around when the Dow Jones created the first stock index? You would be seeing history, and you need to understand that we are in the same spot today. We're about to see history with crypto currency. We are currently being exposed to the same type of trendsetting scenarios, creating new paradigms of the markets.

Chapter 9

Investing vs Trading

We're here to help you remove the blinders so that you can see the information that's been here but hidden, the information that's been hidden in plain sight, to give you a different set of information, to have you begin looking at things differently. Our backgrounds are in investment banking, PhD in finance and economics, and financial advising, but it's not about us. This is about you. Normally you receive financial advice from the person receiving your money, so this is about you having all the information so you understand what it is and what you've embarked upon. So, now, you can take a deeper dive and remove the blinders because this is information that has literally been hidden in plain sight. The wealth shift has been happening consistently, and you now have the opportunity to take advantage of it because now you know about it. When you erase the narrative that's being painted out there, the quote, "They don't want us to have it," when you're referring to the wealthy, or "Other people don't want us to know about it," you'll realize that the reality is that that's not accurate. It is not accurate because the information is there; we just have to learn how we can tap into it. You're here now because you made a decision to do something different. You made a decision to enroll, learn and profit, right?

When you put it into perspective, according to Bureau of labor statistics, the average person makes around $40,000 a year. In order to take advantage of the investments from a healthy financial perspective, my clients needed to make $50-$60,000 a year at a minimum. So why do we do it? Because of what we have been taught. Again, the person taking your money is the person giving you financial advice. I'm not anti-bank, I'm just pro-your-household. I'm not anti-investing, I'm just pro-your-household. I'm pro-education, but so often we get caught up just wanting to be educated. We get caught up on the cliché "education is power". But is that really true? It's not education is power. The question is to ask what are we being educated upon? So it's about having the right information, not just some information, but the right information.

Let's take a deeper look at what the wealthy do. Investing or trading? You understand that both investors and traders are seeking profits in the financial markets and understand how big the financial market is. I really want you to understand how big the market is. The foreign exchange market is $6.6 trillion a day, not including cryptocurrency. With cryptocurrency it's well over $11 trillion a day. So this is the same market you are in, regardless if you're investing or trading. But the difference is the perspective you are taking advantage of it from? So both investors and traders also seek profits through market participation. Understand that when you invest, you invest money with the expectation of achieving a profit. You are literally looking at an investment where you're talking about 10, 20, 30, 40 years that you hold it. If it increases in value, then you can get a nice dividend check every month, or you can sell the value and collect the proceeds, right?

Whether it's for a college fund or whether it's for your actual retirement, or whatever it is for, that's what you're looking for. The goal is to gradually build wealth over an extended period of time. How do you do that? Do you do that by buying and holding? I want you to understand exactly what you are doing when you buy and hold. What you are actually doing is buy and hope. Whether it's stocks, mutual funds, bonds, whatever the case may be, whatever those instruments are, you buy and you hope. Then when you understand, you hold. That means that the transaction is not complete. It's not complete until you actually sell the stock, as an example.

Just envision all the stocks you might possibly own right now. A financial instrument that represents ownership in a company. That means that you have to buy something, you have to analyze the company, you have to see what you're buying, and just pray and hope. You have to hope and pray that you made the right investment and that you didn't get in too late; then you still hope. It's still a good investment. You're doing so much research for that particular company; you're just praying that it rises in value when you're ready to close that transaction.

You're excited when it rises because the market is moving up. But the market moves up and down; it is going to rise and fall, so, if you are just investing, there is absolutely no way you will get excited about a drop in the US30. However, when you are trading, you get excited about movement because you realize you can profit when the market sells as well.

The reality is that most individuals do not have the liquidity to purchase stocks, so they purchase mutual funds. Mutual funds are investments that pool your money together with other investors' who purchase shares of stocks, bonds, and other securities. So, basically, you own a fraction. There are many different stocks that are put into a mutual fund, so it gives the appearance that it's not overall affected by the movement. However, you are still having to invest. You are having to put money up every single month. Every month you're still having to keep reinvesting and you still won't actually own any stock.

Remember, these are your college funds, your retirement plans, and other life events that you've found necessary to plan for. Let's put that into perspective. When you realize that the average person goes back to work after three years of getting their retirement accounts, you begin to realize that the retirement platform that we actually operate under right now with the current IRS codes that govern our 401K, etc., is actually the same plans our parents and grandparents are presently retiring on. In addition, changes in retirement plans have shifted from defined benefit to defined contribution plans. Defined contribution simply means you must contribute to receive a retirement. For example, the military retirement, which was always considered the best retirement plan because you immediately begin receiving your retirement pay at your 20 year retirement and not at your retirement age, is no longer 100% defined benefit. They have shifted to begin including defined contribution.

That change is beneficial to the organization that no longer has to pay out a pre-defined benefit, but in most cases is not to the individual. That is because a) they have to make their own individual choices of where the money is invested, and b) now they are subject to market downturns. Under the defined benefit model, the institution paying the benefit took on the risk. Now, under defined contribution, the employee takes on the risk. So the conversation on how to Be Your Own Bank is so very important to everyone. No one is excluded from the former security blanket that defined benefit used to provide, even though it never provided wealth in the first place.

You are transitioning from a position where you were only able to take advantage of the market when it moved up. You now will be able to do what banks do and take advantage of the market during all movements. Also, instead of holding a position for years before you cash out, you'll be able to cash out immediately. That's why you really have to understand the difference between investing and trading. Now, you will be operating like a bank. It's important to understand the other side of money. That's what we're talking about right now, understanding what it means and what it takes to be on the other side of money.

When you're trading, you take advantage of both the rising and falling markets. You're actually able to exit your positions over a shorter timeframe. The biggest difference is there are no penalties on attaining your money. When investing, you can't touch it until a certain age without penalties. When trading in the foreign exchange market, you have the ability to cash out daily, weekly, monthly or however you choose.

This world has been hidden around you. You've been operating blindly in the foreign exchange market. Have you ever traveled overseas? Have you ever traveled overseas and had to exchange currency? Have you ever seen a currency exchange booth? In this exchange, currency is being bought and sold through the foreign exchange market. There are always two transactions happening and in that transaction profit is being made in the buy and sell of the currency booth. Take each currency booth in the world, plus firms making international purchases, and institutional investing in currencies, and that is the market that you can participate in. Have you ever sat with a financial advisor? If you want a higher return, you put your funds in foreign funds. Do you see how the foreign exchange market is all around you? Now it's time to stop investing blindly with someone else and learn the movement in the market and learn to profit off this movement just like the banks do. Market participants profit off movement and not just when the market rises. It's all about learning when to enter and exit. Investors are content with annual returns of 8 to 15%. When you're trading, you can actually generate 10% each month. So let's learn a skill set that will pay me today and not in 40 years. Right? You have the opportunity to make sure that you are already starting on top. You're already privy to this information because you are reading this book, so why not learn the skillset to trade your money. No, I'm not anti-investing, I'm just pro-you having the right information. Imagine your whole financial understanding to this point and what you've learned thus far in having this perspective. Now you can imagine why we have stayed excited about making sure that our 1 million families are financially educated and impacted. Will I write another retirement plan? No! BYOB is going to help me and you trade because that's what we are passionate about. We want you to understand what the BYOB Movement is all about. We want you to be profitable. Again, we are not anti-bank or anti-investing. BYOB is pro-your-household. Same philosophy, same mindset, same concept. Right information. Right education. Right understanding. Once you know what you're doing and why you're doing it, then you can make your own decision. You can make a decision on how you want to move forward. When you make that decision, you're making that decision from an educated standpoint because your blinders have been removed? BE YOUR OWN BANK!!! Think like a bank! Act like a bank! Be Your Own Bank!

Chapter 10

Think Like A Bank

We want to make sure that we do everything that we can to maximize our information, maximize our awareness, and maximize our profit. The BYOB Movement is an opportunity that is designed to be an opportunity for us to be your RX for Forex and address our economic wounds. Let's be real about it. Money is a very emotional subject. Money is oftentimes an issue that affects relationships. It's something that affects how we feel. It affects our ability to be able to do things. I oftentimes chuckle whenever I hear the Bruno Mars line, "I'm a dangerous man with money in my pocket." We truly are dangerous when we're feeling good and we have the resources to do whatever it is that we need to do. Let's understand that this is not an opportunity for us to have our shoulders tired or be stressed out with the overwhelming feeling of "Oh my God, I have to learn." This is an opportunity for us to recognize how blessed we are to have access to this information. For 25 years, all I could add to someone's life was information, knowledge, awareness, and opportunity to learn something. But now, in addition to that, I can say, "Here's a vehicle. Here's a way in which you can literally begin to bring wealth and abundance into your life."

I really love what the infrastructure is with our Be Your Own Bank Movement because we have the opportunity to be able to understand how to think. **Think Like A Bank!** I went to college with Taraji Henson at Howard University. She was younger than I was, and people used to talk about what a great talent she was and that she had an opportunity to really go far. Well, she did. I'm really proud of her. Every time I see her on television or the movies, I'm extremely proud of her. I bring her up because she has a movie coming out called *Think Like a Man.* The concept of the movie is based on this new perspective and new skill that she develops. She acquires the ability to hear men's thoughts, and she is able to make decisions based on the advantage this gives her. Likewise, the concept here is to have an advantage in my interaction with relationships that I am exposed to by knowing how to think like a bank. We are providing you an opportunity to think like a bank also.

I will give you the opportunity to increase the dynamics of your relationship with money, your relationship with macroeconomic principles, and your relationship with the skill set that goes along with managing your money because we're teaching you how to think like a bank. After studying bank mergers and acquisitions, the actual concept behind the Be Your Own Bank Movement, you will understand that it's bigger than something we just do. To realize that you can do more than just tell people what banks do, you can now provide a vehicle for them to have the same mindset and be able to take advantage of it. The Forex market is a slice of the economic pie. It's an important slice. It's a large potentially lucrative slice, but it is a slice. We need to understand how to put ourselves in a position to master every single part of the economic pie. For example, when we think of banks, we think of the fact that banks are organizations that take deposits and make loans. That's called retail banking. Only 17% of what banks do is retail banking. Only 17% is the function that we're familiar with of them taking in deposits and then making loans. That means there's a whole other world of things that banks do that is part of what makes them the most powerful institutions in the world. Well, that's what we need to do. We need to realize that this slice of the economic financial market pie including the exchange market and the crypto currency market, is absolutely an extremely important slice, but we need to know how to manage the entire pie.

Personal finance is the only area of our society where the people who tell us about it, the people who give us information about it, are the very same people who sell the product.

We need to understand every part of the personal financial model. We need to understand insurance, retirement plans, bank management, investing, and real estate. We literally need to understand every single part of it. You have an opportunity to understand every aspect of personal finances after reading this book today. You will have a clearer picture of what and why you need to increase your awareness. You must get more aggressive about all of the areas of personal finance.

We're going to start with the foundation. We started off being an agricultural world. Everyone who owned wealth measured it in terms of what they had agriculturally, their land, cattle, goats, etc. Think about the book of Job and how the first few verses start telling you about all that Job has. They talk about the fact that he had seven this and seven that. At the end of Job they mention that he has 14 this and 14 that. It's important to note that he doubled what he had even though that's not my point. My point is that it described what he had in terms of agriculture. So that is the world that we used to live in. If everything were agriculture, how did we perform economic functions? We performed economic functions through barter. I take two of your cows; you take six of my pigs. I'll take this parcel of land, and we traded based on that. Good old fashioned barter was the economic way. Even in something as simple as marriage, you would bring a certain level of cattle and exchange it for the opportunity to be able to marry someone's daughter. So that's the way we performed economic transactions.

Finance then became a little more sophisticated. Let's create these coins and place value on them as a certain number of cattle or a certain number of agricultural products. Now let's begin to trade with them. This became more efficient. People were able to carry these coins from one place to another. Then we came up with this paper currency and let the paper currency be backed up by the coins. Technically, the coins and the paper currency are the same thing; one is just lighter than the other. By this time it's now around the 1800s, and we decided for the first time ever we were going to, instead of basing our economic entities on agriculture, for the first time in history, base it on technology. So this was revolutionary. It was so revolutionary that they called it the industrial revolution. So now industry is born. Now we're using technology to make things like steam engines, cotton gins, and railroads. This was significant because everything prior to the industrial revolution in the late 1800s was agricultural based; shopping was simple. You got in your horse and carriage and you rode into town and you bought what you wanted and went on back to the farm. Now with technology, we have conglomerates happening now. So the paper currency was a perfect way to reflect what was going on.

Additionally, banks were born. Instead of paper currency being backed up by coins, it is now backed up by the full faith and confidence of the government. Well, how do we know that it's healthy? We don't. How do we know what's going on behind the scenes? We don't. So two things happened here.

Number one, in some areas, in some countries, in some geographical locations, there were situations where we began to doubt the value and validity of the paper currency. At the same time, the idea was realized that since these currencies are doing different things in different countries, we can trade off of it, which created the infrastructure for what is now known as currency pairs. Currency pairs occurred because one country is doing one thing with their currency and another country is doing something else with their currency, and we can make money off of the difference.

Because these paper currencies are backed up only by the word of these governments and because sometimes there are government entities that may or may not do the right thing, society wanted a more efficient way of monitoring and managing the way economic transactions are done. Well, in the 1990s, we experienced another technological revolution. It was called the Internet. This was not about steam engines and industry; it's about technological innovation. Let's decide to make a currency based on that, and we'll call it digital currency. This is significant, not just because it was the first time that money was created money based on technology. It was significant because of something called the blockchain. The blockchain is nothing but a huge electronic notebook. That notebook allows you to take notes on every single transaction, every single Bitcoin as an example. Bitcoin is a type of digital asset. Any type of Bitcoin, any type of crypto currency that has any action is written on the blockchain. So now we just made the economy more stable. We just made the economy more stable because of our ability to be able to provide a technological undergirding of the economic transactions that take place. We now have a record of everything that happens. The significance of the digital asset means that we have something that has a paper trail that's electronic that will be there forever and will provide a type of currency that the banks do not control.

We just made all the economic transactions become more efficient. One of the things about banks is that banks are control freaks. They love being in control. They love controlling the infrastructure. Have you ever thought about why your check has to be held when you deposit it, and it's a transaction they can do in seconds. But because they control the process, it allows them to always be on the right side of financial transactions. They also said, when you invest, you always want to buy low, sell high, but that is certainly not what they do. They do both sides. They buy low, sell high and sell low, buy high. Basically, whether it goes up or goes down and while they make money. They just call it hedging. As a reinforcement, it is an entire chapter that I cover when teaching a Banking course.

I was in a well-known bank having a business conversation with one of the bankers and the banker said to me, "Okay, you need to be careful." I made a comment about crypto currency, and the banker looked around and said, "You need to be careful about making comments like that because the banking system is now shutting people's accounts down." If they talk about crypto currency, does that mean something's wrong? Crypto currency? No. That simply means that they're not in control of it. So anybody that's taking dollars and rolling it into crypto currency becomes a threat. Think about it. You're able to put your money in a location where you can duplicate it, and it's not in a bank. If you instead have your money in digital assets, it's not in a bank. That is a threat to the banking industry. The gentleman also stated that the bank was also in the process of making digital currency of their own, and they're shutting down anything that deals with any digital assets, but at the same time they see what's going on and they're about to start making their own. The gentleman also stated that it was going to be authorized by the federal government because these original digital assets didn't come from the government. They came from technologically sound individuals that wanted to take matters into their own hands and control the economic transactions between them.

When a digital currency comes out, they raise money also and they do this through ICOs, or initial coin offerings. It's the same thing as an initial public offerings. They are both the same thing; one is with a company, the other with a digital coin. The first time that a particular company decides they want to go public with their stock, they want to have an opportunity to gain more capital by giving up some of that control. Whenever there is an initial offering, there is an investment bank. An investment bank is a part of the banking industry whose job it is to teach companies how to raise capital or to raise capital for them. Think of it as a consultant to help the company to raise money. However, most investment banks feel as though there's too much risk in one bank taking on any IPO. So what they do is they operate in a syndicate, meaning there's several institutions who all get together.

Over the past year there have been several ICOs where banks were a part of the syndicates. So they are telling us that they are not interested in crypto currency; they are telling us that they see cryptocurrency as a threat, yet they are actually on the team behind the scenes making sure that these ICOs come up. So now we've gone from, being anti-crypto currency, to participating in the ICO, to now being financial institutions that are coming up with their own crypto currency in an opportunity to take advantage of this new digital asset trick.

What does this mean for you? The first thing it means is that you need to understand that the wave is moving away from paper currency to digital assets. What you want to do is make sure that you're part of this process, and that you're on this side of the transaction. Secondly, you want to understand that the biggest difference between a currency pair and a crypto currency pair are the fluctuations. How do we profit in this market? We profit in the fluctuations. We all want to understand that we now have another set of data that we can apply the same principles to, and be in profit in the foreign exchange market and the crypto currency market.

The BYOB challenge is real. It's happening and our skill set is continuing to become heightened as we sharpen our

tools even more. The dissemination of information becomes that much more paramount. Think like a bank, act
like a bank, be your own bank!

Chapter 11

Market Psychology

In learning to understanding the market, one thing that is always important to do is understand the big picture. It's always important to understand where you're going and, once we know where we're going and why we're going there, it'll help us understand what we're doing. Then it makes us build on our skillset. It makes the trading skillset a lot simpler. What you're learning is something new; it's not difficult; it's just different. When learning something that's different, you're expanding your mindset for that next level of thinking and the financial paradigm shift in your life.

The market is not random. There is a psychology to it. It's important to understand that we don't and can't shift the market. The market reacts off the emotions of the market makers. We simply ride the wave of the market.

The foreign exchange market is the largest financial market in the world. So that means it's bigger than any market that's out there. This market also repeats itself and moves in patterns. So understanding patterns you understand where it's headed, and you can increase your probability on what is going to or should happen in the future. This will give you a clearer picture of how the market moves.

The market is cyclic. It moves in a cycle. If you look left in the market, it'll help you determine what the right is going to do. Start with a stock, a currency pair, a commodity, or crypto currency. It does not matter. All of them begin to rise with hope: I hope this product takes off; I hope there is a recover. Regardless of the position, it's all hope and faith. The market then transitions into optimism. Buyers are no longer in hope, but they believe that it's real, so more buyers are getting involved in the overall picture. The consensus is, "Is this really happening? Am I really going into profit? Is the market really moving up?" Then belief increases; they move into a sense of excitement. During all of this, everyone is encouraged to buy buy buy, and there is a sense that all are going to be rich—a sense of euphoria. If you can paint a mental picture, the market is on a steady incline. You have to realize that the market is really just going to peak. Think back to the previous chapter where we discussed the roaring 20s, the dot-com bubble in the 1990s, repeal of the Glass Steagall Act, and all the other factors that affect the market. It's a cycle that will consistently repeat itself, and we simply ride the wave.

When the market drops a little and then a little more, our anxiety kicks in. This is what you begin to see on the news. My advice is for you to turn it off. They haven't tuned into the overall psychology, and they are there to evoke an emotion of fear because it brings ratings. They are employed. If it's not financial news, the reality is it's not guiding you towards your financial goals. The market is also going to do what the market does and that is move in a sell position with pullbacks. Remember the pullbacks? Those pull-backs will create denial because you want the market to rise again. You hear statements such as....."Why is the market not pulling back up? What's going on? You know, I'm not understanding." Then, you notice the market is coming down, and it dips in it, and it pulls back a little bit. So, now, they're in denial. They think the market's turning around: "Oh my! These are great companies! It's going to come back!" Think about your emotions. Have you ever seen someone in a relationship and they have been told that the relationship is over, and they are not hearing what the other person is saying? That is what is happening here. The peak is over. You cannot hope, wish, and pray for it to rise again. Once the reality sets in, they panic. When the panic sets in that's when the crash happens because, when people panic, they run, they sell, they get out. They believe it's going to crash and, of course, at this point, it's easy to blame the government: It's going to push it down. So this is what happens. You panic instead of holding. Because you have never been taught how the market moves, you don't have the understanding that the market moves in cycles. The market is going to turn back around and begin this cycle all over again.

This explanation is referred to as "The Psychology of the Market". This is what is happening in the financial institutions where we place our currency. So, understand that it's going to happen. People get angry because they don't understand the psychology of the market. Simplify it; these are things that we learned in school—contraction and expansion. We learned about that in economics class. The psychology of the market is so very important because it's going to peak; it's going to drop, and it's going to recover. Up, down, recover and that the cycles.

These are cycles and now you're seeing the big picture of how this actually applies to the market, the foreign exchange market that you are participating in. It's time to remove the blinders. Understand the cycle and ride the wave because you're in a position to profit from all movement, and not just the peaks.

Chapter 12

Understanding the BYOB Cashout Strategy

Now that you understand the psychology of the market, it's important that you understand how to navigate through the market to put yourself in a position of profit. We want to make sure that with the Be Your Own Bank Movement you're empowered and in a position to win. 1 million families will accept the BYOB challenge, 1 million families financially educated, and 1 million families financially impacted. This begins with you.

Be Your Own Bank is about helping you understand and teaching you how to think like a bank, act like a bank, and become your own bank. In order for us to achieve this goal, in order for us to reach this goal, it means that you have to be empowered. You have to be the one to be able to sit down and execute. You actually have to become your own bank. As we begin to maximize training, and it starts with your saying affirmations, it's important that you have the right mindset. What goes in is what comes out. What's inside of you is what is going to pour out of you. So, it's so very important that when you begin and you start trading, you understand that you are a master trader. You have to say it: "I am wealthy; I am a master trader; all my trades end in profit, and I am the lender and not the borrower." I want you to say this several times a day: "I have ACCEPTED THE CHALLENGE TO BE MY OWN BANK." You are a master trader, and that's the mindset you need to sit down with. That's the mindset that you need to have when it comes to trading. Begin to hashtag #BYOBWORLDWIDE #BYOBCHALLENGE #BYOBCASHOUT. Subscribe to the YouTube Channel BYOB Challenge. You are now part of a community, a community that is changing financial legacies, a community that is reaching 1 million families.

* * *

Everything begins with the right mindset. If you have a clear mindset when you're viewing the charts, that's where you're going to be. So, where we're going to begin is the BYOB Cashout. The BYOB Cashout is built for you to be able to look at three indicators. The strategy was backtested for a year on every currency pair on the 15 min. chart with a 92% accuracy rate. However, I must give you the disclaimer that past profits don't guarantee future success, and also we must account for human error. Additionally, we know that a lot of trading is personality driven. However, in my experience, I recommend that when someone is learning to familiarize themselves with the charts, the lower timeframes help build confidence and comfortability with the market. As you gain your familiarity with the market, you can build on your understanding to implementing the support and resistance lines, trend lines, and other indicators to help you navigate the market to increase your profit margins and begin trading on the higher time frames. We want you to grasp the concept of trading from day one and to also gain a return on your investment. We want to build your confidence in knowing how to trade. We begin our analysis on the lower time frames, "10 pips and cashout", on the 15 min. chart.

Before you understand why the BYOB Cashout works so well, it's important to understand what you're looking at when you look at the charts. Trading is all about finding the proper entry and exit points. The basic foundation of trading begins with a trading process called price action. Price action is simply the movement of the securities price and is the basis for technical analysis. Technical analysis uses the historical data of price and volume to determine future movement. You are looking for an entry trigger based on an area of value. The area of value actually determines if you take the entry trigger.

There are three areas of value that we look at to determine what the market is actually doing at the time. The area of value is a range of prices where the majority of trading volume took place the day prior. That is the trend, moving averages and support and resistance. The trend of the market represents the ups and downs of the prices associated with the currency pair or security. The moving average combines price points over time frames to give you a trend line. It helps determine the trend by examining previous price action. Support and Resistance in the market are predetermined levels of price at which price will tend to stop and reverse. Once in this potential trade area the entry trigger will tell you when to enter the trade. A good entry trigger and area of value will give you a high probability trade.

Additionally, when trading currency, understand that you are always buying and selling at the same time. For example, you have two currencies, GBPUSD. This means that you are trading the British Pound against the US Dollar. The first currency listed is the base currency or the transaction currency. The second currency is the counter currency. The base currency represents how much of the counter currency is needed in order for you to get one unit of the base currency. Based on market strength, if the base currency is the strongest, meaning you believe it will rise in value, you will open a long (buy) position. However, if you believe the currency pair will do the opposite, the base currency will be the weakest and the counter currency will rise in value, you will open a short, or a sell position.

Now that you understand how the market moves, you can apply this information to the BYOB Cashout to further understand its accuracy and how to trade it. The BYOB Cashout uses three indicators. The stochastic, the heiken ashi candles, and the PSAR.

The first indicator we always look at is the stochastic oscillator which is a leading indicator (they anticipate future movement) that was developed in 1950. The stochastic is a momentum indicator that compares a particular closing price to a range of the closing price over a period of time. The sensitivity of the oscillator to market movements is reduced by adjusting the result by the moving average. The stochastic is comprised of two lines; the stochastic slow and the stochastic fast. The blue line is the stochastic fast and tracks the market rate for the currency pair and the red line is the stochastic slow and tracks the last three stochastic blue lines. The stochastic is in a range between 0-100 that shows overbought and oversold conditions. Typically, anything over 80 is overbought and anything under 20 is oversold.

The second indicator is the heiken ashi candle. The heiken ashi candle smooths out price action. The heiken ashi candle is a lagging indicator that is Japanese for average bar. These candles spot trends and predict future prices. The candles make the charts easier to read and analyze. They help with trend identification and reversal. Traders know when to get in and when to get out of a trade.

The third indicator, which is also a lagging indicator, is the PSAR. Parabolic Stop and Reverse. This indicator finds reversals in the market. It acts as a support and trailing stop.

Trading these three indicators together is how we trade the BYOB Cashout. As indicated earlier, we want you to learn trading, and familiarizing yourself on the 15 min. chart and cashout with 10 pips is the foundation of the BYOB Cashout. You will be able to increase your trading and cashout with more pips, but this is the starting point.

Chapter 13

I CAN

We know that we're interested in a better life for ourselves. We are interested in putting ourselves in a better position by learning this skill. We also know that when an opportunity this good, and with this much potential presents itself, we know that we want to share it with the world. I didn't say when we have an opportunity this good, it is an opportunity to make money. What I said is that it is an opportunity to share with the world, and that little shift in perspective, that desire to share it with the world rather than to make money literally puts us in the energetic scenario to make money. It is the energy of wanting to change the world, the energy of wanting to expose someone to something that can make their life better. That literally makes the universe send us the resources to make it happen. So if your goal is to make money, you will make money, but if you want to change lives, the money will come quicker. The money will come stronger because, again, anytime we make a decision to do something that will benefit the world, the universe always is on our side. They are always aligned. They literally will bend over backwards. If you believe that I'm saying it as if the universe is a person, I am, because that is literally the way it functions.

Each one of us represents a slice of the overall universe. Anytime you and I make a decision to do something that will benefit this world, resources are literally sent our way whether we are aware of it or not. You know, it reminds me of a story I heard about Mother Teresa. Mother Teresa is known as one of the greatest Christ-centered individuals, and her ability to be able to change lives and help people was tremendously well documented. There was a situation where Mother Teresa was in a meeting full of individuals that had all decided to get together to do something good for the world and someone in the room mentioned the specific amount of money they were going to need in order to get done what they wanted to accomplish. Someone else in the room said, "Mother Teresa, where are we possibly going to get the funds to make this happen?" She very calmly, as she was known to do, looked over at the individual and said, "The money will come from wherever it is right now." So that very simple but powerful statement just represents my point. Mother Teresa understood that when we have an energy of wanting to heal the world, and we have an energy of wanting to help others, and we have an energy of wanting to contribute to society, the universe bends over backwards to send us the resources. The resources to touch 1 million families, are here, and there's more on the way. We need to walk in the same type of energy that Mother Theresa did. She had a CAN energy. When you walk in a can energy, victory is the only possibility. At no point in our training calls and no point in our Telegram have we ever walked in an energy of CAN not. We always walk naturally without anyone questioning us in an energy of "What can I learn? What can we do? How can this strategy work?" What I would like to do is to reinforce how important it is that we walk in this new energy.

* * *

So, what I've done is taken the word CAN and created a word for each letter that I think will help us to advance our leadership agenda and reach the one million families. We know the BYOB Movement is going to reach them because we have the energy of wanting to heal the world, and, if we are doing something that is a benefit to the universe, the universe will bend over backwards to send us the resources. All we have to do is walk in our CAN energy. The C in CAN stands for Creator. We all are creators. We are creators about business. We're creators of our experience. We're creators about opportunity, and in the same way in which every single religion on earth has a way to explain the way things are created. We need to walk in that same energy. Often times, certain ways in which we're taught in business, in organizational America, are to educate ourselves and passively wait for an opportunity to come, but we need to recognize who we are. We need to know that we are walking in our life force energy that literally is the creator of worlds. Think back to the song "Wind Beneath my Wings." The song is literally saying that I can fly. There's a certain wind that you get from your situation, a scenario that will bring energy into your life and make you fly even higher and soar to new heights. Realize we are the wind beneath our wings. We have to create the opportunities. I know you've taken positive action. Listen to all of the wonderful things that are being shared though the BYOB Movement; then take those words and use them to create your own opportunity. So right now I want you to be real with yourself, and I want you to think about the last seven days. Ask yourself how many times you created an opportunity. Then ask yourself this question, "What can I do over the next seven days to ensure that I am creating, that I am making something happen?" Are you taking an action step that will create something because we are all little creators. We create our own earth. We create our own experience. Let's take our leadership to the next level and think about and be about how we can create opportunities.

The A in CAN stands for Achiever. We literally want to put ourselves in a position where we take great wisdom and knowledge that we're being exposed to and think about how we can achieve, how can we get to the next level?

In striving for achievement, we seek the best practices that we can do, actionable steps that we can implement to help us achieve. One of the things that I've been doing recently to help me achieve is buy a large dry erase board which I put right in front of my laptop. Then, while I'm sitting at the laptop, I can see it and I can add things. So every single night I write down all of the things that I want to achieve for the next day. Now, whether you are aware of this or not, studies show that we release endorphins when we put forth this effort to achieve these goals. Endorphin is a chemical we all have inside of our body that, when released, makes us feel better. It's the feeling that we get when we have a new date or a new love, the feeling we get when we're holding a baby, or the feeling we get when we eat our favorite food. Every time you cross something off of your list, you release endorphins.

So that's the beauty of us coming together in the BYOB movement. I want you to see yourself as a creator. I want you to see yourself as an achiever because then you can talk about creating, but it's a verb that you have to go and do. If you are a creator, it's part of who you are. It's a label that's on you. For example, did you have a nickname when you were a child? Let's call you Pookie. When you're a child, it's cute. However, when you're in your 50s, you want your peers to refer to you by your first name but they still call you Pookie until you're 87 years old. Ha Ha funny! But you've been labeled. The name you put on yourself is who you will be. So I purposely made you a creator, and I purposely made you an achiever.

C is for creator; A is for achiever; and N is for Narrator. Narrator is someone who tells the story. A narrator is someone who in novels, television, or the movies is explaining what's going on, giving the feelings, talking about the decisions, and describing everything that's going on. Thinking about the significance of a narrator, there is a show on Netflix called *Dear White People*. On this show there is a group of African Americans at an Ivy League college campus. There is a narrator that from the very beginning of the show has been describing it. In Season Three, one of the concepts is the characters meet the narrator and want to kill the narrator. However, this point is not about the show, but about the narrator. Try to understand why they would want to kill the narrator. What could possibly be the point? So you can tell your own story! Kill the narrator because the narrator is the one that's creating the narrative of how things are for you. But when you recognize that you are the narrator and that you are the one telling the story and creating the story, achieving the achievements, you've now taken power. You're taking responsibility for your own power. If you don't like the events taking place in your life, you change the channel. Just like if we were watching that show mentioned before, we would change the channel; we would not keep watching it. You are the narrator.

* * *

Sometimes leaders, sometimes business builders, sometimes even be your own bankers experience something that happens, a story where there's a situation where this someone says something to them or does something to them that they perceive as being wrong. They keep talking about it and talking about it and attract situations that are wrong because that's where their focus is. That's where their energy is. That's what they're thinking about. That's what their awareness is. So we have to understand the power of being our own narrator. You are the one who is telling your story. What are you saying to yourself when nobody is around? Are you your own cheerleader? Are you telling your story in a positive light for yourself? Are you telling your story in a way where you feel good, where you're the hero at the end of the story? Are you narrating in such a way where no matter what the situation is, you win? You have to really do some soul searching about what you're saying to yourself?

So, to me, it's so important that we understand that C stands for creator. We are the creator by experience. It's so important that we recognize that we are an achiever and we want to operate in best practices where we're consistently achieving and putting ourselves in a position to continue to achieve. But most importantly, we want to think about the story we're telling ourselves as a narrator. Are you telling a story of success? Are you telling a story of can do it? Are you saying to yourself, what if they can't? What story are you telling?

Write the vision and make it plain. As you are writing these things down, speaking it into existence, your belief level increases, accelerating this process. Also, in a multiplicative fashion, everyone's belief levels increase because you're experiencing your own story, creating an ability, achieving it now. Now you're narrating your story. One million families financially educated and impacted. That begins with you.

Chapter 14

The Lion & The Lioness

Only about 15% of the population is aware that they can trade in foreign exchange. So, let's look at that as a tremendous opportunity. That means that there's 85% of the world that we can go to and we can share this information with, that we can spread this gospel to. Where will it start? It starts with you.

Your RX for Forex—why do we call it that? It's because we recognize that there are some prescriptions that can be written to help us understand our financial situation to a higher degree. To help us understand that we have a very unique opportunity right here, you're literally hearing from individuals whose backgrounds have been exposed to this information. Mr. Gerald D. Rogers is the visionary behind the Be Your Own Bank Movement and has a background in investment banking. Ms.Tasha M. Dyer has a back ground as a licensed financial advisor and is the creator of the BYOB

Cashout trading strategy. Dr. Craig Bythewood is the Finance Doctor, over 26 years of experience as an educator, Chief Financial Officer (CFO) and consultant.

For the past 26 years you've been doing some very important things, but it just so happens that I was being exposed to some material which can help you with two things: first, in your quest to be your own bank and, secondly, to economically empower your household to understand all of the components of the personal financial pie so that you can ask the questions that you need to ask to put yourself in the best position to manage your money, to have a mindset about money, to have a positive relationship about money.

Ms. Dyer frequently says, "You want to have a relationship with the market." She often says that the market will talk to you if you listen to it. Ms. Dyer gives the analogy of having a relationship with someone and making sure that you're listening to them because she recognized that sometimes in the heat of emotion we listen to respond instead of listening to listen. That's a really good point. Remember, how you do one thing is how you do everything. Apply this concept to your life and you'll know if you are applying it to trading. There is a technique called mirroring that can help you implement this concept in your life and trading. If two individuals are having trouble listening to each other because they're so emotionally charged and ready to answer, the mirroring technique works like this. You have someone say something. Then when they finished talking, the other person has to mirror back what was said. Then the person that said their original statement has to give them credence that yes, that's what I said. If they don't get it right, then they have to do it again until they get the statement right. Then the person who gets the statement right can now say what they want to say. When that person speaks, then the next person has to mirror what they say. This mirroring techniques takes all of the emotional charge out of it because, eight times out of 10, the person listening gets the statement wrong. Why? Because they're so ready to say what they have to say. This is a technique that works. Use it with your children when they have an issue, but more importantly, use it when you have an emotional situation or you have an emotionally charged topic. Use it to listen to the market.

Additionally, you want a relationship with money. Money is a tool. Money is a currency. Money is an energy. If you think about it, just for a second, how has your relationship been with money over the last 10 years, 15 years, and 20 years? You'll probably recognize some patterns. If money is your friend, it'll do like your other friends do. It'll always find you and want to hang out. If money makes you tense, people don't like being around tense people, and now that they're also tense, the energy is off. So you really need to think about the relationship that you have with money because it makes a difference.

How you view something and the energy associated with it is important. For example, I have been a professor for 26 years. In my classroom the word confusion is not allowed to be said. One of the things that I noticed is that confusion, just like money, is an energy. I've noticed that if someone says to me in a classroom setting, "I'm confused," when I give them the answer, it takes them a while to receive it because the energy of confusion is stronger than whatever answer I'm providing.

If you've ever taken a class with Dr. Craig Bythewood, you would notice when you walk in there the first day that on the board there is the word confusion and that it has one of those circles with the / through it that says you're not allowed to say that. So one of the things that I do in my own ground classes is that I call it the C word. The reason why I call it the C word, the reason why I disallow them from saying it, is because I recognize that confusion is an energy. When you are aware that confusion is an energy, it doesn't matter what is said; it doesn't matter what situation is going. So think about it. Say the word confusion and watch how it makes your shoulders tight. Confusion, confusion, confusion, tightens your shoulders up. On the other hand, watch how light you feel when you say this word Clarity. So, it's not about someone trying to dictate to you what you should say. It's about understanding the fact that there's an extreme and distinct difference between the energy of being confused and the energy of wanting to understand.

Everything is energy and you have to shift your mentality. What you resist will persist. So when you push against something, you're literally bringing it into your experience.

Babies respond off your energy. If a baby is crying and you get tense while trying to calm the baby down, the baby cries more because it's feeding off of your energy. But when you're calm and you say, "Okay, okay, come here; it's okay," that baby calms right down. When a toddler falls, he or she looks up to see your reaction. If you jump and react, they start crying, but if you say, "It's okay, get up, shake it off, you're good," he or she does exactly that. So what I'm saying to the baby or the toddler, they're just examples of the way in which energy works. When you have a desire to understand something and you walk in the energy of understanding and wanting clarity, guess what? You get understanding and clarity.

So really take this seriously because, not only is this about confusion, it's about other ways in our life where we may be talking about what we don't want. When we find ourselves in this situation, we have to pivot. Identify where you want to change, where you need to make a shift in your life, where you want to make a change, and this is where you pivot. This is the concept that we can use to make sure that we're walking in clarity and understanding rather than walking in confusion.

When you find yourself saying or thinking or operating in a vibration of what you don't want, you have to identify what you don't want in order to identify what you want.

How would you know that you want something good, unless you've experienced it? How would you know that you want hot if you haven't experienced cold? So, literally, I get the fact that we have to first identify what we don't want. The issue is, as humans, we identify it and then we stay there. We keep talking about it, we keep repeating it. We keep using all of this heavy language and this heavy energy and guess what? We stay there! We have got to learn to manage energy. We have got to learn how to pivot. We have got to learn how to change direction. So, the moment you feel yourself saying something, thinking something with a heavy energy—I'm confused. I don't get it. I don't understand. I don't know how this is going to do—and this may happen, anytime you hear yourself thinking and speaking in a language that you do not want, just pivot.

In fact, I want to give you a technique that you can use right now because, once I share this with you and you hear me, when you go back into your normal situation, this is a way to trick yourself into pivoting more often. The human brain does not know the difference between imagination and reality. This is a technique called the two-for-one technique. Anytime you catch yourself saying or thinking anything with a no in it, anything that represents what you don't want, anytime you catch yourself saying that, thinking that, immediately respond with two positive statements. For example, if you say to yourself, "I might miss my flight.," come back and say, "I'm going to make my flight. I'm going to make my flight." If you say, "I don't like this," come back with, "I love this. I love this." It doesn't even have to be the same thing. You're just responding to whatever NO statement you make with two positive statements. It's very easy. You have to be very aggressive with it. It has to be two. No thinking. Just do it. It is just that easy. I hate that. I love this. I love this. You can even use pronouns. I don't want to do that. I want to do this. I want to do that. Now think about it. If you use this two-for-one technique, at the end of the day, you will have insured that 66% of the things that you've thought and said were positive. Two for one. When you catch yourself saying, "I'm confused. - I understand, I understand," "I don't like this. - I love this. I love this," "I don't want to do this. - I want to do this. I want to do this," 66% of the time, which, of course, is more than 50%, you're speaking life into your existence; you're talking about what you want. Guess what; your experience will match that. It is spiritual and physical law.

So think about what we're doing right here; this is the Be Your Own Bank Movement; you're developing the skill of being able to participate in a $6.6 trillion dollar-a-day market. We're literally taking steps to become the King of our jungle. We're literally putting ourselves in a position where we can roar into a new abundance level and by reaching out and helping touch one million families, we really have the opportunity to be the King of our families, to be the King of our community, the King of our social groups, and the King of our work groups. I love lions and there is a huge picture of a lion in my living room. So this lion is a very, very important symbol to me personally, but it really represents where we are and what we're doing as a movement.

* * *

I took the liberty of taking the word lion and thinking about some concepts that I think are relevant to where we are right now. Let's take the word "LION" and let's think about some words that can accurately reflect what we need to focus on as we continue to take our trading to the next level, as we continue to take our mindset to the next level, as we continue to have a relationship with the markets, as we continue to have an outstanding relationship with our money.

Lion is spelled L. I. O. N. The L stands for Learn. Mr. Rogers is always referencing how important it is to understand that this is an educational platform. We should focus on the fact that we're here to learn a skill. So the L in LION stands for Learn.

What are we learning? We're learning to do something that's a little bit above and beyond what we may have done in the past. If we think about our parents, we have to think about our grandparents also. If we think about the last two generations, we've gotten away from putting money away, and we have focused on spending. So, rather than focusing on spending, let's instead focus on that. I'm standing for invest because if we invest, we have the ability to be able to spend more. So L stands for learn.

The I stands for Investing. We're learning to invest in $6.6 trillion dollar-a-day market, and, when we include crypto currency, over $11 trillion dollar market a day, and we are learning to invest.

O stands for Optimistic. Confusion is the opposite of optimistic, clarity in understanding. I am a master trader; all of my trades in profit. We start every one of our trading sessions with that by design because it's optimistic.

L stands for Learn. I stands for Invest. O stands for Optimistic. What does the N stand for? In this instance N stands for two things. We're going to take the N-word and make it positive because we are absolutely taking our mindset to the Next level and it is Non negotiable because now that we're here, that's it. There's no going back.

We are about to drill ourselves into learning this information and putting ourselves in the best position to get to the other side of wealth and abundance. At this point it's non negotiable. L stands for Learn. I stands for Invest. Best O stands for Optimistic. N stands for Next level and Non negotiable. The picture that I can see in my peripheral vision is a picture of a lion, a male lion with a big mane. It is the King of the jungle. But if you ever wondered why he's called the King of the jungle, I can tell you because I'm an Animal Planet nerd. The reason that he's called the King of the jungle is because he doesn't do anything. You know why he doesn't do anything? It is because of who does the hunting? The lioness does the hunting. So, if I could be real for a second, appreciate the power of a woman, the power of feminine energy. Get it; understand it. In order for men to be the King of the jungle, the lioness has to go out there and hunt. Do you not see that Mr. Gerald D. Rogers and Dr. Craig Bythewood benefit because Ms. Tasha M. Dyer goes out there and hunts. She hunts for the best indicator. She hunts for the best trade. We all eat because she is a lioness, and she's hunting. She's always on the hunt, and we appreciate her for what she does. So, me being the lion, I am going to recognize it. It's about the lioness. So, if it's going to be about the lioness, we have to add three more letters. L stands for Learn. I stands for Invest. O stands for Optimistic. N stands for Next level and Non negotiable. . But now let's add the E, the S, and the S, yes, because it's all about the LIONESS.

The ES is about the Exceptional Skill that you and I are learning by participating in this skill. You and I are learning an exceptional skill. Do you realize that we just learned how we can take everything we've learned on the 15 minute time frame and compare it to the hour time frame. That simply means that we've increased our ability to be able to make money. We've increased our ability to be able to increase our PIP count. That's an exceptional skill. L stands for Learn. I stands for Invest. O stands for Optimistic. N stands for Next level and Non negotiable. E S stands for Exceptional Skill. So, we pay homage to this feminine energy that goes out there and hunts for what the men need. They hunt for the comfort; they hunt for the motivation; they hunt for the ability to make us feel at home.

So the lioness stands for L. I. O. N. E. S., but there's one more S, and this S is so important to who we are and why we're here. This S is so important to what the Be Your Own Bank Movement is. This S is so important to what females do in our lives. Can you imagine what your mother did to put you where you are? Can you imagine settlers, the women in their life that make the sacrifice to do what it is that you want to do? No, S is not sacrifice because that word is heavy. The second S stands for Selflessness. Selflessness. When we have the ability to be able to put others first, we, by design, have the ability to capture the power of the universe and propel ourselves to higher and higher heights. Of course, we have to care about ourselves. I flew twice in one weekend, and each time they said the same thing, "In case of an emergency, place your oxygen mask on first and then help others." We're here to develop our skill. That's why Selflessness is the last S, because once we develop our skill, once we put on our abundance oxygen, once we walk in our economic swag, then we have the ability to help others, to take this message to one million families, to help those individuals around us, to teach our children how to invest in an eleven trillion dollar industry. L stands for Learn. I stands for Invest. O stands for Optimistic. N stands for Next level and Non negotiable. E S stands for Exceptional Skill. S stands for Selflessness. Let's take on the image and the power and the strength of the image and let's be kings of the information. Let's continue to hunt and let's put ourselves in the position we need to take ourselves to all of our goals, to all of our desires. We are reaching one million families through this economic empowerment vehicle and through our selflessness.

Chapter 15

WomenTEACH4x

The WomenTEACH4x movement is designed to impact women's lives around the world. To understand this movement, one would need to know the foundation that it is built on and the importance of participation.

This is the WomenTEACH4x launch and you might have heard some of the buzz or it being referenced, but in order for one to capture the essence of WomenTEACH4x, revelation must be shined upon the past, present, and future of the woman as a whole.

But in order for us to be a true movement, in order for us to really impact lives, in order for us to truly make a change, I just feel and I believe that it's very important that each and every last one of us who has embraced and those that will embrace the BYOB movement and the cause, understand the foundation.

Allow me to share my story. I'm no different than any of you. No different than any woman that is out there, no matter our locations, our backgrounds, or how different our situations are; regardless of what you went to school for, what college degree you obtained; whether you went straight into the workforce, military; regardless of whatever you did, we are the same.

We all have the same goals as far as being successful and creating our individual footprint in life. We have families, dreams and desires that drive us towards success. As a woman, you have to have endurance that a man doesn't because you will face obstacles that are specific to being a woman. Women face things that men are not able to fully understand. Even if they strive to deal with what we face and attempt to walk in our shoes, as women we have been conditioned to survive. We are the backbone of the family. We are the connectors. We are the glue. We are the source, resource, and consistency of the family. Regardless of the family size, income structure, or circumstances, the woman's role is significant. We are smart, resourceful, and very significant. Most things that are advertised and marketed are geared to women, such as beauty products and skin care, which are superficial things. Yet the truth is that God created us beautiful, yet we are also intelligent! We are educated; we have degrees, and we are ingenious. There is so much we have and can accomplish, but the playing field is not level. Equal pay is still an issue and will be for at least 100 more years at a minimum. So what do we do? We take control.

* * *

So who is Tasha M Dyer....

U. S. Army Major retired, MBA, Financial Advisor, but I am a woman that has faced the same obstacles as every other woman. I just chose to rise up and deal with what happens in life. I am a woman that had a vision and refused to become a statistic. I grew up the oldest of three children in a single-family household with a mother who was chronically ill and who has since passed away. While in high school I had to transfer out of a magnet program and could not participate in sports and missed many school activities because my sister and I had to work to help keep a roof over our head. I moved to Atlanta for college and had to return home because it was not financially feasible. I had my first child at the tender age of 20 and found myself joining the military immediately afterwards.

When you think about these experiences, I was in a dark space. Being a pregnant teenager at the age of 19, I was in shock for allowing myself to get into that situation and everyone who knew me was as well. I was the only freshman in the history of my college to achieve an internship opportunity with the Department of Defense for the position I had applied, and now I found myself not able to engage. I was told over and over again that I would be a statistic by members of my family. That was crushing. I was told I was the one that was supposed to make it out. That was discouraging. There was so much negative energy coming my way because of the situation that I allowed. I had an aunt to even offer to pay for an abortion and another one offered adoption. That was terrifying to me. I do not believe in abortions, and I would never consider giving up my child to someone plus watch my child being raised from afar. With this array of emotions, I slipped into a depression. Thankfully, hope shined, and I saw a light when another aunt offered to pay for my education and move me into her home which allowed me to finish school while she assisted in the caring for my beautiful daughter. That offer alone gave me a revelation that sometimes all women need is someone to give them hope. Women need someone to lift them up and give them the light of Christ and the understanding that there is more to life. I began to always operate in optimism. It is not when the movement officially began, but it's when it began within me.

I entered the military as an enlisted Soldier, and, when I made the decision that I wanted to become commissioned, I submitted my packet to become a commissioned officer. An officer in my section that had never spoken to me before and had no approval or denial authorization submitted a letter of disapproval just because I was single parent. My parental status was not part of the approval process. Obviously, I got commissioned, but it was a fight I should not have had to fight.

This was my ultimate choice of career, but later on in my story, while deployed to Kuwait, in support of Operation Iraqi Freedom and in charge of two major operations that were imperative to the Iraqi drawdown, my caregiver decided she didn't want to allow me to speak to my children. I went months without having communication with my children. Leaving a deployment was not an option. At the end of the deployment, when we were returning to the states and as I was planning to go get them, the caregiver decided to put them out, and I was given an emergency leave. As an officer in the United States Army, this was not favorably looked upon to have inadequate family care, and I lost an opportunity for a command position, a senior management position, that I had already been selected for. To this day my children have a bond that is unbreakable with one another, yet as their mother I had to regain their trust. I was in a situation as a woman and a mother where I had to choose between my career and my family. Ultimately, I chose my family, but the process was not quick or easy. I also caught a lot of backlash behind my career decisions.

As a civilian I actually interviewed for a company to start up an HR department and was hired after several rounds of interviews with the owners of a company because I had an MBA and experience. When it was time to solidify pay, I placed a number on the table with increases over the next three years. They wanted to pay me $10,000 a year less than that. I did not accept the position, and later on I found out that the job was given to a less qualified male with no previous job experience other than serving two years in the military for the same pay I requested.

I can elaborate with story after story just as I am sure many women can, but all of this is to let you know that life happens and you are either going to happen to life or allow life to happen to you. But what has come from this is a movement, a movement for women by women because we will face things that men never will.

So many have learned how to survive and continue pressing on. In this cycle of life you get the homework done and the food on the table and just keep pressing in this cycle of life where women just focus. Women have endurance, a natural nurturing spirit, where we are not allowed to shut down; excuses are eliminated, and we just make things happen.

It's time to stop and be able to make a choice to live life on your terms. It's time to stop surviving and start thriving. It's time to live the dreams that you once dreamed of as a child, the dreams that God is still speaking into you. Remember, we are all the same. We all have a dream, a vision, and a story. It's time to level the playing field. This is why WomenTEACH4x was birthed.

We have an opportunity to not only create equal pay but also exceed it because we can create our own value. Relying on someone else to do it will never happen. It does not happen even when you work harder; it only happens when you work smarter and focus on making a difference and making an impact. I've spoken with so many people, and this is the story that you hear. We as women have so much to get accomplished, and we cannot continue to ignore that a choice has to be made. Our children, spouses, bills and everything else is waiting for you to do so.

Hearing so many stories; so many obstacles, I could not walk away and turn a deaf ear. I'm sure you hear people say things like, "You know what? We can't; I can't, or you know I'm going to figure it out; I'm going to make it; I'm going to make it work; I'm going to stretch a dollar; or I don't have the funds or resources." If it's not the finances, it's the career, and you don't have the time with your family that you desire. WomenTEACH4x was born just for us because it's time for us to stick together in unity. We have to build each other and empower one another. This is a better way.

The path BYOB, Be Your Own Bank, is a platform where the information that has been hidden in plain sight is now available to you to participate in this evolution of currency and learn a skillset to think like a bank, act like a bank, and become your own bank. What is happening and what's going on is the banks are using our money and BYOB helps you transition into becoming the bank of your own life.

* * *

WomenTEACH4x.

What does "TEACH" mean?

The T in TEACH means to Transform your mindset. So your mindset is key. As a man thinketh, in his heart, so he is. Everything we do, we have to stop and think. Transform your mindset to understand that there is a market that is larger than the credit market, the largest financial market in the world. So we want to transform your mindset because we take pride in everything that we do as women. We take pride in our homes, we take pride in our families, in our children. When we are married, we take pride in our spouses; we are so grateful and thankful.

But what about our finances? It is often where we're stretched regardless of what our bank account looks like. Whether it is $5, $500, or $5,000, our level of living and what our expenses are, along with what our expectations are meet our standard of living. So $5 to somebody might be $5,000 to somebody else, but it's still the same and the finances are where we often get stretched. We want to eliminate that, and we do that through transforming our mindset so we actually think differently about money.

Now that you are thinking differently, you are ready for the second letter. The E in TEACH is for Empower. You'll invest in yourself by accepting the challenge to Be Your Own Bank and you will be empowered with a life changing skill set, tools, resources, coaching and mentorship to excel. Finances are normally the main area to address and this movement empowers you to obtain that and much more.

Appreciate is the A in TEACH. Appreciation is one thing that we women need to hear, feel, and know. We do so much. We sacrifice consistently. Being a part of the WomenTEACH4x movement, the appreciation culture is just contagious. Each woman reaches out and shares with others the enjoyment of recognizing the great qualities observed.

The C in TEACH is commitment. We have to begin to commit to ourselves. How you do one thing is how you do everything. So I want to paint a picture. If you've ever flown before you'll be advised if you ever need oxygen you must place the mask over your face before you can help someone else. If you don't, you'll run out of oxygen. Your labor will be in vain, and you won't be able to save yourself or your loved ones. This same concept has to apply to your life. That's why I began with how you do one thing is how you do everything. In life we so often try to commit to everything but ourselves. We make time for everything but ourselves then wonder why things fail or don't work out. Society would have us believe that we are selfish if we commit to us first. I am here to challenge your thinking. You need to commit to yourself first. The same way you're sitting on that airplane and you must place the oxygen mask on your face first to survive and assist others is the same concept you have to apply to life. That is when you become whole and when you are whole is when you can help others. That's when you give the best of you to your families, your communities, your church, your friends, your jobs, and anything else you are involved in. It must start with you! Commit to yourself and your future.

The final letter in TEACH is H. The H stands for honor. We want to honor you. We want to honor each individual woman. That's what we want to do because we want to lift your crown. We want to let you know that you are respected and you are loved. Each woman is wonderfully and beautifully made as a child of God. So if we lift up each other and pour into each other, pulling each other towards success, there won't be room for failure. We can remove those barriers that chip away at women and cause division and destruction.

This is WomenTEACH4x. Transform your mind. It's time to think big and unleash what's inside of you to manifest. It's time to embrace something new. It's time to change the trajectory and learn a skillset and create profit. It's time to take the mental shift from the consumer and give yourself permission to change your life.

One million families, one million women financially educated and that begins with you!

Tasha M. Dyer

Chapter 16

Accepting the BYOB Challenge

The foundation has been laid. You understand the concept, and the blinders have been removed, information that you have been exposed to your entire life but you were unaware of. Now it is time to make a decision. You will see the BYOB Movement all around you, the same way you see the Nike logos. You will meet the BYOB Mastermind team and the authors of this book: Mr. Rogers has a background in investment banking and is the spokesperson of one of the company tools that we represent; he brings credibility and understanding that we are using software that is comparable to what the big banks of the world utilize. Major Dyer has a background as a financial advisor and the creator of the BYOB Cashout that has individuals profitable around the world. Dr. Bythewood has his PhD in finance and economics and was the first African American to receive this degree from the University of Florida and the 11th in the nation at the time. His dissertation was on bank mergers and acquisitions. We present this information to you because a true financial education is something that we are never educated about, and we are here to shift that paradigm. Don't let your finances be the only thing you aren't properly educated on.

* * *

Be Your Own Bank....the Movement

* * *

The Largest Economic Empowerment Movement in the History of Mankind
One Million Families Financially Educated & Impacted

WomenTEACH4x, BYOB Millennials Owning Banks, Faith & Finance,
BYOB Males2Men, Boots2Banks

ENROLL~ LEARN~ PROFIT!!

Accept the challenge to learn how to BE YOUR OWN BANK!!

When you're on social media pull up the hashtags #BYOBChallenge #BYOBCashout #BYOBWorldwide & YourTube subscribe to BYOB Challenge

BEYOUROWNBANKMOVEMENT.COM